BRIGHT NOTES

OUR TOWN AND OTHER WORKS BY THORNTON WILDER

Intelligent Education

Nashville, Tennessee

BRIGHT NOTES: Our Town and Other Works
www.BrightNotes.com

No part of this publication may be used or reproduced in any manner whatsoever without written permission, except in the case of brief quotations in critical articles and reviews. For permissions, contact Influence Publishers http://www.influencepublishers.com.

ISBN: 978-1-645425-06-9 (Paperback)
ISBN: 978-1-645425-07-6 (eBook)

Published in accordance with the U.S. Copyright Office Orphan Works and Mass Digitization report of the register of copyrights, June 2015.

Originally published by Monarch Press.
Francis R. Gemme, 1965
2020 Edition published by Influence Publishers.

Interior design by Lapiz Digital Services. Cover Design by Thinkpen Designs.

Printed in the United States of America.

Library of Congress Cataloging-in-Publication Data forthcoming.
Names: Intelligent Education
Title: BRIGHT NOTES: Our Town and Other Works
Subject: STU004000 STUDY AIDS / Book Notes

CONTENTS

1)	Introduction to Thornton Wilder	1
2)	Introduction to The Cabala	10
3)	Plot Analysis	12
4)	Character Analyses	18
5)	Essay Questions and Answers	27
6)	Introduction to The Bridge of San Luis Rey	30
7)	Plot Analysis	33
8)	Character Analyses	39
9)	Essay Questions and Answers	48
10)	Introduction to Heaven's My Destination	52
11)	Plot Analysis	54
12)	Character Analyses	60

13)	Essay Questions and Answers	70
14)	Introduction to Our Town	73
15)	Plot Analysis	96
16)	Character Analyses	110
17)	Essay Questions and Answers	127
18)	Introduction to The Skin of Our Teeth	134
19)	Plot Analysis	138
20)	Character Analyses	145
21)	Essay Questions and Answers	147
22)	Critical Opinion	149
23)	Suggested Research Paper Topics	153
24)	Bibliography	156

THORNTON WILDER

INTRODUCTION

Thornton Niven Wilder is one of America's most respected contemporary authors. His writing has been far from prolific, but what he has published is a fresh interpretation of age-old themes, presented in a modern idiom and a concise prose style. In contrast to many of his contemporaries, notably Ernest Hemingway, John Steinbeck, and John Dos Passos, he is like the man in Rudyard Kipling's "If" - he kept his head while those around him were losing theirs, especially during the decade when they were all literary apprentices and the center of American literary life was in Paris. Today Wilder lives in Hamden, Connecticut, where he is working on his latest drama, *The Seven Ages of Man* and *The Seven Deadly Sins*, two cycles of one-act plays. The many honorary degrees and lectureships, three Pulitzer Prizes, a Gold Medal from the Academy of Arts and Letters, and the warm reception of his works, particularly *The Bridge of San Luis Rey* and *Our Town*, have been well deserved laurels for an artistic career which spans four decades. On May 4, 1965, Thornton Wilder was awarded the first National Medal for Literature at a White House ceremony.

EARLY LIFE

Wilder's father, Amos, earned his doctoral degree in economics at Yale and entered upon a career in journalism. He first edited the *Journal* in New Haven and then went to Madison, Wisconsin, where he edited the *Wisconsin State Journal*. It was in Madison that Thornton was born on April 18, 1897. He was given the family names of his mother, Isabella Thornton Niven Wilder. The second of five children, two boys and three girls, Wilder spent the first nine years of his life in Madison. His home life was characterized by a strong religious and intellectual atmosphere which allowed him to read widely, a habit which has been the main influence in his career.

Because of his support of Theodore Roosevelt, Amos Wilder was appointed American Consul General at Hong Kong and Shanghai. In China, Thornton attended a missionary school at Chefoo. The Wilders returned to America in 1910 and settled in California, where Thornton attended high school at Berkeley and prepared for college at the Thacher School in Ojai, California. It was during this period that the young student became enamored of writing and wrote the three-minute play, *The Angel That Troubled the Waters*, which was published in 1928.

COLLEGE DAYS

Entering Oberlin College in 1915, Wilder studied the classics, and continued to write plays. After two years he transferred to Yale only to leave college the following year to enlist in the Coast Artillery Corps. His older brother, Amos, who was also destined to become a writer and teacher, saw service in the ambulance corps as did Hemingway and Dos Passos. Upon completion of his tour of duty, Wilder returned to Yale to complete his B.A. in 1920.

In his two years at Yale, Wilder's main activity was the Yale literary magazine. In addition to writing short stories, plays and reviews, he also composed and played music on the piano. He was described by one of his professors as a quiet, modest, attractive student, alive with literary ambition. He published his first full-length play, *The Trumpet Shall Sound*, in the "lit" during his senior year.

Following graduation Wilder studied archaeology at the American Academy in Rome. He then accepted an appointment as an instructor in French at the Lawrenceville School in New Jersey. Wilder was associated with Lawrenceville from 1921 to 1928. In addition to teaching, he was a housemaster, but still the literary ambitions of his college days allowed him to write forty three-minute plays, earn an M.A. from Princeton, and publish two novels.

THE WRITER

The Cabala, published in 1926, was the result of his impressions in Rome several years before. It was dedicated to his friends at the American Academy. In 1927, he published *The Bridge of San Luis Rey*, which made his famous almost overnight. It was reviewed favorably, sold widely, won a Pulitzer Prize, and gave him enough income to allow him to quit teaching.

He now entered formally upon a writing and teaching career which has included three additional novels, *The Woman of Andros* (1930), *Heaven's My Destination* (1935), and *The Ides of March* (1948), and three major plays, *Our Town* (1935), for which he won his second Pulitzer Prize, *The Skin of Our Teeth* (1942), for which he won his third Pulitzer Prize, and *The Matchmaker* (1954), which was a revision of an earlier play,

The Merchant of Yonkers. The Matchmaker was also made into a motion picture, and, recently, used as the source for the popular Broadway musical, *Hello Dolly*.

After leaving Lawrenceville in 1928, Wilder spent two years in Europe studying continental drama. In 1931, he accepted the invitation of Robert Hutchins to become a lecturer at the University of Chicago. He taught for six months of the year and wrote for the other six. Since 1936, he has directed his full efforts, except for *The Ides of March* (1948), toward the stage.

During World War II he served with the United States Air Force in North Africa and Italy. Since the war he has continued lecturing at many colleges, universities, and cultural centers in America and abroad.

SOURCES AND THEMES

The three principal influences on the writings of Thornton Wilder are his religious background, his love of classicism, and his worldwide travels. The settings of his novels range from Rome of the 1920s in *The Cabala* to the Rome of Caesar in *The Ides of March*, from the Greece of pre-Christianity in *The Woman of Andros*, to the mid-Western American corn belt of Kansas in *Heaven's My Destination*, and finally to colonial Peru in *The Bridge of San Luis Rey*. In contrast the settings of his plays are the representative small town of Grover's Corners, New Hampshire in *Our Town,* New Jersey in *The Skin of Our Teeth*, and New York City of the 1880s in *The Matchmaker.* To Wilder, "the proper study of mankind is man." There are set in America and whose characters wear modern dress and speak in modern idiom. Wilder himself has acknowledged his debt to many writers. Part of his artistic credo is the analogy that literature is like a torch race where one writer passes the literary flame of ideas on to another, very much in the fashion of Olympic runners. Among the writers who have influenced his work are the classical masters. Sophocles and Virgil and the more modern authors, Marcel Proust and James Joyce. As a writer, many critics compare him to Henry James.

His philosophy of writing is not to create something new, but rather to restate the old verities in a clearer and more modern way. His background is easily seen in many of his works by his use of Biblical, classical, and archaeological motifs and allusions. If there is one **theme** which unites all of his works, it is humanism. To Wilder, "the proper study of mankind is man." The two most obvious motifs found in his works are love in all its dimensions and time, the framework within which all men live. Wilder watches a clock of human history and while, as are all men, he is concerned with the present, he nevertheless sees the spectrum of all history and the daily events of the present in archetypal perspective.

THEORY OF DRAMA

In "Some Thoughts on Playwriting," which appeared in the *Intent of the Artist* (1941), Wilder presented his theories on drama. Briefly, he said that drama differs from the other arts in four ways:

First, drama depends on many collaborators - the dramatist, the actors, the director, and the audience. A dramatist should write so as to take advantage of the attributes of an actor. An outstanding actor must first of all be observant, secondly be imaginative, and third have the physical qualifications to play the role.

Secondly, drama is addressed to the combined mind of an audience. Therefore, the scope of drama must be wide enough to appeal to a majority of the people experiencing it. To capture the audience, the main technique must be action and movement.

Thirdly, drama is a pretense. It must appeal to the general and imaginative experience of the audience. Therefore, little elaborateness or spectacle is needed.

Fourthly, Time in a play is always in the present. Unlike the novel which tells what happened, a play tells what is happening.

Finally, Wilder points to the greatest periods of literary history, in particular The Golden Age of Pericles and The Elizabethan Age, both of which produced the greatest dramas the world has ever known, to show the scope which drama can attain and to indicate why he turned from the writing of novels to the writing of drama.

Nearly fifteen years later, in "A Preface to Three Plays," Wilder commented more directly on why he turned from writing novels to writing plays. Because of their lack of **realism**, he became disenchanted with the dramatic productions of the late 1920s. Yet he felt that drama was the greatest of all literary forms. Complacency, conformity, and gentility had turned the stage into an unreal place of artificial sprites. Drama needed archetypal dimension, a creation which represented contemporary man as one with all men at all times. The clothes, customs, speeches, and names of men may have changed during two thousand years, but human nature, with its problems and dilemmas, successes and failures, triumphs and tragedies, had not changed. To live was no tragedy, but to live and not to love or not to experience life was the greatest of tragedies.

HIS DRAMATIC THEORY APPLIED TO OUR TOWN

Evidence of Wilder's dramatic theories can be found in all of his plays. Let us expand *Our Town* within his critical requirements. First, drama must have universal audience appeal. *Our Town* takes place in Grover's Corners, New Hampshire, a typical and fictional American small town. The setting is one which would be familiar to almost any American audience. A paperboy, a milkman, a soda jerk, a high school baseball hero, the church organist, and the country doctor are a few of the characters whose faces are familiar to a small American town at the turn of the century. Universality can be seen in the proper names Wilder gave his characters. The principal families in the play are the Webbs and the Gibbs; yet so as not to limit the appeal of *Our Town* to a white-anglo-saxon-protestant majority Wilder mentions other ethnic and religious groups which go to make up any typical American sociological cross section. And where do these minorities live? Across the tracks, naturally!

Our Town also fulfills Wilder's requirements for pretense and time. There are few props: a table and a few chairs, two ladders, and two stools. These props are used for a majority of scenes in the Webb's and Gibb's homes. The ladders represent at one point in the play the second floor rooms of George and Emily; they also are used for the two stools at a simulated drugstore counter. At the end of the play the dead sit in two rows of chairs which represent their final resting place.

The Time is the present in *Our Town*. The stage manager, as well as the players, tell us what is happening. In chronology, *Our Town* begins in 1901 and ends in 1913. It covers the three life cycles of love, marriage, and death. It achieves archetypal dimension by the commentary of the stage manager who questions this same cycle in the daily life of a Babylonian George and Emily two thousand years ago. We soon discover that love and marriage and death have been a common experience to all men in all ages, and will probably continue to be so.

A successful production of *Our Town* does demand the collaboration of observant, imaginative, and physically gifted actors. In a matter of less than three actual hours they must play roles which cover thirteen years. Let us consider for example the role of Emily Webb. At the beginning of the play she is a teenager, in the second act she is a bride and in the third act she must play the role of a dead person, and yet for a moment use the voice of a girl of twelve when she relives her twelfth birthday. As is true of most drama, *Our Town* in the hands of an unobservant and unimaginative actress would appear ridiculous and unreal; yet in the hands of a gifted actress it would achieve the dramatic success it deserves.

SUMMATION

In comparison with other writers of his era, wilder seems quiet and reserved. His writings do not indicate the isolation of Sherwood Anderson's Winesburg, Ohio, nor the passion and soul searching of F. Scott Fitzgerald or Ernest Hemingway, nor the social or economic criticism of John Steinbeck or many other proletarian writers. His quiet **satire** in *Our Town* and *Heaven's My Destination* does not begin to approach the devastation wrought by Sinclair Lewis' *Main Street* or *Elmer Gantry,* novels on similar themes. Wilder was criticized for a time because he refused to allow his characters to become embroiled in contemporary social issues. But as a student of archaeology and history he had probably reasoned out all he had to say about America's economic crisis of the 1930s when he studied the rise and fall of Rome.

Only time, one of Wilder's favorite themes, can judge his place in American literature. While his contemporaries seemed to dissect the flesh and blood of the American character, Wilder was busy examining the heart and soul. As some literary historian is sure to comment in some future age, it does, after all, take all of these elements to create a total personality, even a fictional one. Wilder is a humanist of the first order. He considers love as the basic need and ingredient of the good life. A Greek and Augustan sense of proportion permeates all his work, stylistically philosophically, and critically.

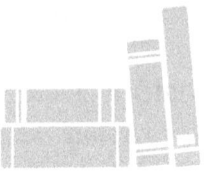

THE CABALA

INTRODUCTION

The setting of Thornton Wilder's first novel was drawn from his experiences in Rome at the American Academy. It includes many of his experiences during his archaeological studies in the Eternal City in 1920 - 1921. The time of the story is 1920; the length of the action is one year. The structure of the novel is built around a young American writer, Samuele, and his relationship to the Cabalists, an affluent group of aristocrats. Without these two unifying elements the novel is merely a group of fine realistic character sketches.

For one of his main motifs, Wilder borrowed Virgil, Dante's guide in the *Divine Comedy,* to resolve his questions at the end of the story. It is this element which makes the novel a fantasy rather than solely a novel of manners. Wilder begins by describing Virgil's land, which his young narrator says he has dreamed of visiting for eight years. He makes several references to Virgil within the narrative also. For example, M. Bogard chooses not to say anything controversial, but rather wants to talk of the Church or Virgil. In her first encounter with James Blair, Princess Alix d'Espoli is impressed with his long recitations from Virgil. Even in the seance scene there is an **allusion** to Virgil's still being alive.

the main theme of *The Cabala* is the final end to the old pagan gods. It is not, however, until the end of the story that we are given a direct comparison by Miss Grier. But early in the story, when Blair first tells Samuele of the Cabala, the writer looks forward to meeting these "Modern Olympians." Also early in the story, a young Roman socialite describes them as sitting off in Tivoli, a modern Mount Olympus, and exercising their powers. Even the astute Mme. Agaropoulos says there is something supernatural about them. Their personality traits - pride and fickleness - align them with their counterparts of mythology. At one point in the story Samuele draws a lengthy analogy, without using specific names, between the traits of the Cabalists and the traits of the ancient gods.

The story begins idealistically with a young and somewhat naive young man visiting romantic Rome for the first time. Its central portion is a realistic description of several memorable characters. Its end employs a fantasy in which the classical voice of Virgil tells us to put our faith and dreams and efforts in the New World and not in the old one.

THE CABALA

PLOT ANALYSIS

BOOK I - "FIRST ENCOUNTERS"

James Blair, a young American archaeologist, and Samuele, a recently arrived young American writer, are traveling by train from Naples to Rome. The railroad carriage contains the usual continental assortment of travelers. Blairs tells Samuele about the Cabala, a group of powerful and aristocratic Romans who spend their time influencing political, social, religious, and intellectual matters. Blair says that his friend Mrs. Agaropoulos feels the Cabalists are bored conservatives and traditionalists who resent anything that's modern. She feels that they are almost supernatural. Blair lists the Cabalists as Miss Grier, an American millionairess, Cardinal Vaini, the Princess d'Espoli, the Duchess d'Aquilanera, and a Mrs. Bernstein, a semi-retired directress of a major German banking firm. Each, he says, has a phenomenal gift. Blair tells Samuele that he will arrange an introduction for him to Miss Grier.

Arriving in Rome, Blair helps Samuele find an apartment. They spend a few days furnishing it and Blair hires Ottima to cook for Samuele. At a social hour given by Mrs. Agaropoulos,

Samuele meets his first Cabalists, Miss Grier. Samuele is alert enough to know that Miss Grier is making some sort of political bargain with a Mrs. Roy. Miss Grier invites Blair and Samuele to one of her regular dinner parties. At dinner Samuele meets Marie Astree-Luce de Morfontaine, another Cabalist. Astree-Luce tells Samuele of her desire to have the Church proclaim Divine Right of Kings as dogma so that France would once again have a king. Samuele dismisses her as odd. Astree-Luce invites Samuele to spend the weekend at her villa in Tivoli. At the insistence of Miss Grier, Samuele decides to accept, reflecting that in Rome friendships are formed rapidly. Besides, Astree-Luce has a great favor to ask of him. In the course of the evening, Samuele has asked Ada Benoni, another of the guests at the party, about the Cabala. Donna Benoni feels that they are a group of malcontents bound together solely by common interests; they influence indirectly and subconsciously, rather than by any direct means, in social, political, and religious causes. Their battlefield is the dinner table; their parliament is a weekend gathering at some villa. Before leaving, Miss Grier insists that Samuele return for a midnight supper. She tells him she has a great favor to ask of him. The young New Englander, so recently arrived in Rome, feels it is strange that these mighty international aristocrats would seek favors from him.

Blair and Samuele visit a sick and dying poet who is bitter over life. The poet resembles John Keats, and represents an artistic sympathy between an old writer at the end of his career and a young writer at the beginning of his.

BOOK II - "MARCANTONIO"

Samuele meets Duchess d'Aquilanera at Miss Grier's midnight supper. She recalls the former days of her great family, but now they have little social status. However, she plans to marry her son, Marcantonio, into a fine and prestigious Roman family. However, Marcantonio is only interested in the sweet life of free women and sports cars. The Duchess wishes Samuele to lecture her son on the harms of such a libertine life. Samuele has been chosen because he is from New England, where morality is a way of life. Somewhat hesitant, he nevertheless agrees, with the urging of Miss Grier, to attempt to reform young Marcantonio. He will visit the Colonna Villa after his weekend at the Villa Horace, the palatial home of Astree-Luce.

A few days later Astree-Luce sends a car for Samuele. It contains M. Lery Bogard, a famous historian, who is also a weekend guest. They have an evasive conversation as the young idealist refers to some of the controversial writings of M. Bogard's early days. Samuele resents Bogard's apathy and conservatism. Activity at the villa is in the grand tradition of affluent aristocracy; the only major activity of the day is dinner. Samuele also meets three more members of the Cabala, the Cardinal, Madame Bernstein, and Alix, the Princess d'Espoli. The Cardinal draws Samuele aside and offers him his summation of Marcantonio's problems. Samuele, while impressed with the achievements of the Cardinal's life, sees him as a worldly cleric who is only interested in Marcantonio's maintaining a superficial morality. Upset by this conversation, Samuele decides to abandon the reformation of Marcantonio. But he is reconvinced by the charming Princess d'Espoli. Soon Miss Grier arrives and takes Samuele outside to meet Marcantonio. At once haughty and selfish, Marcantonio takes Samuele for a ride in Miss Grier's sports car. They talk of America and Marcantonio's goal to run in the 1924 Paris Olympics. When they return from their ride, Samuele notes that the entire Cabala is interested in Marcantonio's salvation. Returning to Rome, Samuele is bothered by Mr. Perkins, a tactless Babbitt whom he met on a boat when crossing the Atlantic.

Samuele leaves with Marcantonio for the Villa Colonna. At dinner he meets Donna Julia, Marcantonio's half sister. The two young men spend their days playing tennis and their evenings talking of track and physical conditioning. Toward the end of the week, the vain Marcantonio turns to his sexual prowess in one of their talks. This allows Samuele an opportunity to refute his host's way of life. Through a blend of Puritan morality and modern psychology, Samuele actually puts the fear of God in him. Visibly shaken that night and still highly resolved the next day. Marcantonio moves like a man transformed. The next night he awakens Samuele at a late hour to tell him he was right. In jumping over the wall of the villa early the following morning in an attempt to crash the party, the Babbitt, Perkins, discovers Marcantonio's body in a flower bed. He has committed suicide.

BOOK III - "ALIX"

The Cabalists receive the news of Marcantonio's death philosophically. The Duchess feels that it was due to his sudden acceptance of morality. She lauds Samuele for his efforts. Samuele comments that he has come upon the Cabalists in the middle of their decline. While they still influence minor religious and political issues, they have little power to combat the rapidly rising forces of the twentieth century, especially Fascism and economic crises. He next turns his attentions to the beautiful and vivacious Princess Alix d'Espoli. Her external joy is only a facade for her unhappy marriage. She also suffers from one major flaw - she always falls in love with someone who cannot possibly love her. She soon falls in love with Blair. Tragedy is imminent. They are complete opposites; Blair is an introvert, escaping life by burying himself in the minutiae of antiquity; Alix, on the other hand, loves to squeeze the essence out of every moment of life. Alix becomes frustrated by awkwardly throwing herself at

Blair at every opportunity, always without success. Blair rudely ignores her and buries himself deeper in the trivia of history. His life is one long series of classical footnotes. He resolves to go to Spain to protect his freedom. Samuele attempts, as best he can, to console the depressed and masochistic Alix. Despite his warning, Blair returns to Rome and accidentally meets Alix at a seance. She is so shaken that after an aborted trip to Greece she suffers a complete mental breakdown. Samuele remains close to her until she is well on the road to recovery, although he knows she will never be over her love for Blair.

BOOK IV - "ASTREE-LUCE AND THE CARDINAL"

When Samuele visits the Villa Horace, the magnificent palace of Astree-Luce de Morfontaine, he soon learns that she is not only a religious fanatic but also a monomaniac. She lives only to see a king reign in France once again. Her piety and sincerity convince Samuele to help her in this project, which is already a century behind the times. Her plan is to have the Church proclaim as dogma the Divine Right of Kings. The significance of this is that after such a proclamation, Roman Catholics would believe that God rules through the monarchs on earth and that they are influenced by Him directly. To commence her plan, she needs the help of Cardinal Vaini, whose faith and intelligence could easily influence the Vatican. With such a decree, the faithful of France would most certainly restore the monarchy. Samuele visits the Cardinal, only to find a bitter, worldly, and faithless man. Perhaps his twenty-five years of mission life in China have finally taken their toll. In a personal confrontation with Astree-Luce, the Cardinal, using his superior rhetoric, easily shakes this pious and faithful woman. She becomes so unstable that a dinner the following week, she makes an attempt on Cardinal Vaini's life. Samuele is horrified at the incident. The Cardinal, like Tennyson's *Ulysses,* desires to return to the site of his former victories and fame. He receives permission to return to China, but dies of fever en route.

BOOK V - "THE DUSK OF THE GODS"

Samuele now reflects on the fate of the Cabala as he is about to leave Rome. He visits the Cardinal's sister and the grave of Marcantonio. Astree-Luce has gone back to France to spend her days in seclusion, and he cannot bring himself to visit Alix and perhaps open old wounds. He spends an afternoon with the Duchess d'Aquilanera and learns of Donna Julia's forthcoming marriage to an Italian nobleman. He spends his last evening as he had spent one of his first - in a long conversation with Miss Grier. They talk of the Cabala, and she tells him that they are the ancient pagan gods reincarnated in human form. Samuele doubts her word and becomes even more skeptical when she tells him that he, too, is a young god - Mercury - the messenger of the gods. As Samuele is sailing home, he invokes Virgil to unravel these puzzling events of his year in Rome. Virgil laments his own belief in the Eternal City, stating that it is but transitory compared to heaven. It is but one Rome of many Romes before it and the many more Romes which will follow. His final advice to his young admirer is to drink the full cup of Rome's magic and then choose a younger city, one that a young man can help to create and build, not an old one like Rome where you can only exist in the golden days of the past.

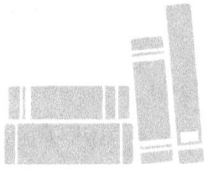

THE CABALA

CHARACTER ANALYSES

SAMUELE

The narrator of the story is a young American writer who is a confidant of the Cabala. He was waited eight years to come to Virgil's land. He meets all the Cabalists, becomes involved with them, and hints at their being pagan gods risen again. His feelings are confirmed by Miss Grier at the end of the novel. Samuele is somewhat of a social opportunist, exhibits the ethical values of the New England Puritanism of his ancestors, and displays a fine knowledge of antiquity. He is an avowed lover of Virgil and shows a good sense of polite humor. Structurally, he is the unifying element in the novel. Miss Grier, on the eve of his departure from Rome, tells him he is an incarnation of the ancient god Mercury. In many respects Samuele is a fictional Thornton Wilder in Rome; he reflects the aspirations, insights, and sensitivities of a young artist.

JAMES BLAIR

An archaeologist and Samuele's friend, Blair tells him about the Cabala and later introduces him to Miss Grier. He has studied classics at Harvard for six years and came to Sicily to advise a motion-picture company. When the company failed, Blair wandered throughout antiquity. We never learn why he is trying to escape life, but he has little to do with the living and spends his time filling huge notebooks with archaeological trivia. He rudely rejects Alix when she falls in love with him, and retreats further into a haughty egotism to protect his independence.

MISS ELIZABETH GRIER

An American millionairess and Cabalist, she was the sole heir to a railroad fortune. Insecure from her childhood, Miss Grier had a compulsive need for company. She is the epitome of the intelligentia. She is in the habit of giving midnight dinners and imploring her guests to stay all night. When they decline, she assuages her loneliness by listening to little known pieces of classical music played by a troupe of musicians kept on hand solely for that purpose. She is fluent in three languages and considered a busybody by most Romans. Eventually, she tells Samuele that the Cabala is the ancient gods incarnate and that he himself is the god Mercury. Her statement is probably influenced by the manuscript which she is currently reading, in which ancient gods are reincarnated.

CARDINAL VAINI

This Prince of the Church, a Cabalist, is eighty years old. He is Vatican secretary in spite of himself. As a brilliant and rebellious seminarian many years before, he had chosen the mission field of China rather than the theo-political arena of Rome. Through intelligence, imagination, sacrifice, faith, and prayer, his success in China was not overlooked and he was made a Bishop. His fame as the Churchman of China has spread throughout the world and he enjoys as much popularity and as many visitors as the Pope. Soon he is elected to the college of Cardinals as a result half of admiration and half of fear. He has little trust of his fellow clergymen. In turn, he is despised for his brilliance and forthrightness. However, he spends his last days in bitter disillusion and without faith or joy. He enjoys reading literary contemporaries. It is his worldliness and lack of faith which causes Astree-Luce to make an attempt on his life. After this he attempts to return to China, the scene of his greatest theological triumphs and personal joy, but he dies while on the way. His power and influence are comparable to that of the ancient god Zeus, but his gifts of wisdom and understanding are soured by becoming ensnared in the politics which he so studiously tried to avoid earlier in his career.

ASTREE-LUCE DE MORFONTAINE

A Cabalist, Astree-Luce is a religious perfectionist in an imperfect world. She attempts to shoot the Cardinal because of his worldly philosophy. She also hates him for his inertia and his refusal to support her grandiose plan on behalf of European royalty. She lives for one goal, to have the Church proclaim the Divine Right of Kings as dogma. Since she is of royal lineage herself, she naively feels such a dogma would cause the faithful of France to restore a monarch. On the positive side, she is truly pious and humble and an active philanthropist. At first Samuele dismisses her theory as a century behind the times, but, as always, he becomes involved. She represents the traditionalist role in the novel, and her faith, unsupported by reason, is also symbolic of an earlier age and way of life.

ALIX D'ESPOLI

A Princess and Cabalist, Alix has had an unhappy marriage and has lost two children. She is delicate, fashionable, and a genius at conversation. Her major fault is that she always falls in love with someone who could never possibly love her. Time after time, including her thwarted affair with Blair, she hurts herself by loving an inferior. She suffers a mental breakdown before finally learning to live without Blair's love. In *The Cabala*, Alix is representative of the love-goddess, Venus, who must struggle on without her love, and yet never is really the same again.

THE DUCHESS D'AQUILANERA

A Cabalist, she is first regarded by Samuele as a witch. She is fifty years old, short and lame. She comes of old and proper royal ancestry, but her line has fallen on bad times in recent years. She lives solely for the restoration of her son, Marcantonio, and daughter, Julia, to their proper place in society. Her plan is to accomplish such a restoration by a proper marriage. Marcantonio is a disappointment to her, but his final attempt to change from his worldly ways brings her some satisfaction. She rationalizes that his suicide was the result of his rapid moral transformation. She represents an outworn aristocracy that has not yet given up its hope of again achieving its social pinnacle.

MARCANTONIO D'AQUILANERA

The vain teenage son of the Duchess, he causes her no end of anxiety because of his libertine friends, affairs, and interests. He began well in school and in social life, but soon became the victim of his licentious life, much to the dismay of the Cabalists. The interest of the Cabala in Marcantonio springs from the fact that he represents their progeny, and it is for him to carry on their ideals. His love of freedom and lack of responsibility associate him with the boy-god, Pan.

JULIA D'AQUILANERA

Marcantonio's half-sister, she is cold and stiff with Samuele, but constantly teasing and frolicking with Marcantonio. Samuele believes their relationship is not normal. She fulfills her mother's desire when she becomes engaged to an Italian nobleman at the end of the novel.

MADAME BERNSTEIN

A minor Cabalist, she is the power behind a major German banking house which she directs through her sons. She loves music, and the Cabala gives her an opportunity to forget her successful career of earning money and to indulge in her second love - music.

MRS. ROY

A lobbyist at the Vatican for charitable organizations, Mrs. Roy appears as a character representing what is good and uncomplicated in human nature. But behind her philanthropy is her desire for a papal title and a divorce under the Pauline Privilege. She bargains with Miss Grier for the latter's influence in her divorce proceedings. In return Mrs. Roy lobbys on behalf of Vassar College, of which Miss Grier is a trustee. She uses her influence to reconcile a forthcoming scandal over a valuable Italian painting which had been stolen and recently presented to Vassar.

M. LERY BOGARD

A scholar and historian, Bogard wrote negatively early in his career of certain aspects of Church history. Elderly now and a member of the esteemed French Academy, he avoids controversy and seeks constant conciliation with the Church. He terms his early heterodoxy as youthful indiscretion. He associates with the Cabala by invitation, and represents the lack of moral courage of the older writer as opposed to Samuele's avid desire to learn and to seek the controversial.

MRS. AGAROPOULOS

A patron of the arts, little known artists, and vagabond intellectuals, she is a friend of Blair. It is at Mrs. Agaropoulos' party that Samuele meets his first Cabalist, Miss Grier.

FREDERICK PERKINS

A businessman from Detroit, he met Samuele on the crossing. After exhausting his own political and financial influences in visiting Italy for the first time, he pleads with Samuele to introduce him to some real Italians. He discovers the body of Marcantonio as he is crashing the Villa Horace at seven in the morning. He is the worst of the Ugly Americans and the best of the Babbitts.

ADA BENONI

The young daughter of a popular senator, she tells Samuele some interesting points about the Cabala.

VITTORIO

He is Ada Benoni's fiance.

OTTIMA

Ottima is an intelligent, middle-aged Italian who is hired by Blair to cook for Samuele. Her companions in the kitchen are Kurt, a police dog, and Messalina, a cat.

ALVIERO

He is Astree-Luce's faithful servant.

Comment

When it was first published in 1926, *The Cabala* received little critical attention. Stylistically, it was a model for its economy of words, elimination of nonessentials, and kernel or epigrammatic sentence structure. This is seen when his detailed descriptions of characters or scenes are often followed by short, direct (epigrammatic) sentences expressing some universal truth or observation.

Style and characterization are the mainstays of the novel. The fact that the reader is not overly upset by the fantasy scene at the end of the story attests to the emphasis on characterization. Virgil is a natural choice for an oracle. But Wilder had too much sophistication to make a specific analogy between an ancient god and his modern counterpart in *The Cabala*. His only exception to this is when Miss Grier identifies Samuele as Mercury, the messenger of the gods. Like Ishmael or the ancient mariner, Samuele would carry his tale far and wide. The other deific comparisons, he leaves to the reader.

Critics and readers have easily identified Marcantonio as Pan, the son of Mercury and god of the woods. Pan symbolizes freedom and lack of responsibility. The Cardinal is associated with Zeus, the father of the gods, Miss Grier, with Minerva, the goddess of wisdom, and finally Alix and Blair with the ill-fated lovers, Venus and Adonis.

The Cabala reflects the three major influences of Wilder's career. The narrator is well versed in his own New England Puritanism, the philosophies of materialism and scepticism, and the many hues of Vatican Catholicism. Classical **allusions** are plentiful, sometimes as archaeological asides, but most of the time as a layman's Baedeker to Rome. An autobiographical strain is evident as the major influences of religion, travel, and the classics appear.

Symbolically interpreted, the book has a general meaning and several specific ones. The major **theme** is that the ancient gods have had their day. The relationship between the Duchess and her son could easily symbolize the destruction of an older aristocratic order by the onrush of individualism and the implied results of social and economic equality. The conflict of Cardinal Vaini and Astree-Luce clearly is a battle of faith and reason. In a parallel conflict, Alix's freely-given love and sacrifice are abruptly and coldly rejected by Blair who represents the inhumanity of science and technology.

At the end of the novel, when Virgil tells Samuele that Rome is merely a pinpoint in the scheme of time which has been seen before and will be seen many times in the future, he is expressing a major **theme** of Wilder's philosophy.

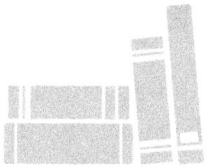

THE CABALA

ESSAY QUESTIONS AND ANSWERS

....

Question: What does the word "cabala" mean, and how it is related to the story?

Answer: "Cabala" means an esoteric and secret group. It is synonymous with clique. The group of aristocrats which Samuele meets in Rome is a clique which influences social, political, and religious issues. They meet at each other's villas, at recitals, and for dinner parties. They like their roles as the powers behind the scenes. Included in the group are Miss Grier, an intelligent American expatriot who seems to be the organizer; Cardinal Vaini, an outstanding missionary in China and now in a high position in Vatican circles; Mrs. Bernstein, a German millionairess; the Duchess d'Aquilanera, the epitome of the aristocrat tradition; Marcantonio, her son, a wastrel; Astree-Luce Morfontaine, a royalist who desires the monarchy returned to France; Princess Alix d'Espoli, the lovely one of the group, socially adept and sparkling especially at conversation. The "Cabala" influences issues more through inaction than direct intervention. Together they are feared and despised by most of the Romans. But these same Romans always weigh what the Cabalists will feel about a certain project. For example, they are able to block Rome's purchase of a certain group of paintings and a new museum. The decision of the Cabala is arrived at many times as the result of whim or selfishness. They do not do this formally or in any legislative way, but people are always afraid of what they will say if a decision is made against their judgment. Samuele has come upon them in the twilight of their power. Their power steadily wanes throughout the story, especially when they are confronted with the new economic crises of the twentieth century. For example, they are powerless to influence the labor movement or the rise of the Fascist party in Italy.

Question: What is the relationship between the narrator and the Cabalists?

Answer: Samuele, the narrator, is a young American writer who is introduced to the Cabala by his friend Blair. He becomes involved with Miss Grier when she asks him to do a favor for the Duchess d'Aquilanera, another Cabalist. Somewhat hesitant, Samuele is convinced by Miss Grier, the Cardinal, and the Duchess to try to reform Marcantonio, the Duchess' libertine son. Although the boy commits suicide, Samuele is praised by the Cabala for his attempt to change Marcantonio. The Cabalists call the narrator Samuele. He has no other name in the story. They are amused by his youthfulness and foreignness. Alix compares Samuele to an eager hunting dog; the Cardinal compares him to a Boswell; the Duchess says his eyes shine because he comes from a new and rich country. The fact is that Samuele is accepted by the Cabalists because he loves them, and their individual conceits cannot resist flattery and attention. In the middle of the story, Samuele is intimately involved in the thwarted love of Alix and Blair. He becomes a therapist to Alix during her depths of depression and heights of nervous anxiety. In the latter part of the story he visits the Villa Horace and sees that Astree-Luce is more than a political extremist or religious fanatic; she is truly sincere, pious, and penitent. On her behalf he visits the Cardinal and finds him to be a bitter, disillusioned old man. His first and last acts with the Cabala are visits to Miss Grier. Visiting her on the eve of his departure from Rome, he is uneasy when she calls him the reincarnated ancient god Mercury. In the final fantasy in the story, he is advised by Virgil to dedicate his life to the new world. Interpreted symbolically, Samuele, representing the new world, becomes involved in some degree with each of the Cabalists who represent the old world. In the final scene Samuele returns to America somewhat wiser and more experienced.

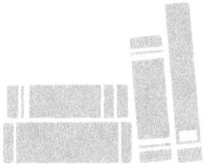

THE BRIDGE OF SAN LUIS REY

INTRODUCTION

The Bridge of San Luis Rey, Wilder's second novel, was published in 1927, a year after *The Cabala*. Whereas *The Cabala* met with a fair critical reception and moderate success, *The Bridge of San Luis Rey* was hailed in glowing terms by the critics and the reading public. It became a best seller, won the Pulitzer Prize, made Wilder famous, and was later made into a movie.

The action of the novel centers around a single incident - the collapse of an old footbridge in Peru in the early eighteenth century and the deaths of the five people who were crossing it at the time. The title of the first Chapter, "Perhaps An Accident," states part of the philosophical paradox explored to a certain extent in the novel. The title of the last chapter "Perhaps An Intention," states the second half of the proposition. The preliminary consideration is one of life's basic enigmas, "Do we live by accident or by design?" The three middle **episodes** which constitute the bulk of the novel give detailed accounts of the lives of the five victims. The question of chance or design is raised by Brother Juniper, a Franciscan monk who witnessed the **catastrophe** and attempts to reconcile such events within the framework of theology. The narrator draws his biographical material about the five victims from an old manuscript in which Brother Juniper assembled the factual and anecdotal material for his investigation.

The question of whether we live by accident or design is universal, since we need only open our daily newspapers or listen to the latest news program on radio or television to find parallel incidents in our own experience. A plane crashing, a ship sinking, a school bus overturning can be considered topical examples which Brother Juniper would question. We can usually tell why such things happen, at least on the mechanical and technical levels, and even on the level of human error - the pilot misjudged, the ship captain was careless, the bus driver had a heart attack - but we still wonder why it had to happen. Why do thousands of innocent people die in these **catastrophes** all the time? This is the question Brother Juniper sets out to answer.

The story is told by a narrator in an omniscient point of view. In the first chapter, the narrator tells us that to attempt such an investigation into the lives of the victims to determine whether or not God is just would be skepticism for most of us, but because of Brother Juniper's faith, sincerity and theological training, there is nothing wrong with his asking the question. Using a familiar fictional technique, the narrator tells us that he happened upon a secret copy of Brother Juniper's findings in a large volume he discovered in the University of San Marco library. The original copy was burned as was Brother Juniper for heresy many years before. But for six years Brother Juniper had assembled notes about the lives of the victims until he finally amassed what he considered a logical case for their deaths. The narrator warns us that perhaps Brother Juniper missed the real meaning of their lives and perhaps even the narrator will never understand the true nature of the victims. Perhaps, concludes the narrator, it is not meant for us to know whether our lives are governed by design or accident.

The story takes place in the early eighteenth century in Peru, when that country was a Spanish colony. In a varying degree, all of the lives of the major characters are interwoven and their lives lead the victims in the natural course of their travels to the bridge at the exact moment of its collapse.

Stylistically, *The Bridge of San Luis Rey* shows Wilder at his best. Like *The Cabala,* it is a model of economy with no incident or description which is not essential to the whole work. The depth of detail and the ironies of coincidence allow us to view the characters as living people rather than only as figures in print. The epigrammatic sentence is basic to the style. The first and last sentences in the novel are as famous as any found anywhere in American literature. The first sentence of the story states the time, place, number of people involved, and the incident which motivates the story's being told. The last sentence of the story, expressed by the Abbess, is a kernel of philosophical truth, and, perhaps, the only finite answer possible to the infinite nature of the questions asked by Brother Juniper.

THE BRIDGE OF SAN LUIS REY

PLOT ANALYSIS

PART I - "PERHAPS AN ACCIDENT"

On the road between Lima and Cuzco in colonial Peru, there stood an ancient foot-bridge, which travelers used while their wagons and baggage traveled several hundred feet down the gorge to cross the stream on small rafts. The bridge was woven of vines and built by the Incas. The small chapel near it and the bridge were named for St. Louis of France, and it seemed the bridge had stood for ages. However, on July 20, 1714, the bridge collapsed and hurled five travelers to their deaths. The travelers were the Marquesa de Montemayor; her maid, Pepita; Uncle Pio and his ward, Jamie, the illegitimate son of La Perichole, a famous actress; and Esteban. A humble and pious Franciscan monk, Brother Juniper, witnessed the disaster and resolved to investigate the lives of the victims in an attempt to determine whether man's life is determined by accident or design. His six-year investigation and the character sketches of the victims constitute the major portion of the story.

PART II - "THE MARQUESA DE MONTEMAYOR"

Dona Maria, the Marquesa de Montemayor, who was to become famous in Spanish literature for her letters, which became a model of the language and times in which she lived, had an unhappy childhood. She preferred to remain single, but at twenty-six she married a brokendown nobleman. A beautiful child, Clara, is born to this marriage, and the child becomes the center of the Marquesa's life. As a result of her own miserable personality, the Marquesa and her daughter are incompatible, and the child takes the first opportunity to remove herself to Spain by marrying a nobleman. An attempt at reunion fails four years later when the Marquesa visits the Spanish court. Thereafter all relations with the only person she ever loves are left to the ideal world of the Marquesa's letters to her daughter. The Marquesa becomes more active in Limean society so that she will have things to write her daughter. She ignores the fact that her daughter does not love her.

While attending the theatre in hopes of securing some material to include in her next letter, the Marquesa is insulted by Camila Perichole, the greatest actress of the day. The actress is forced by the Viceroy to apologize to the Marquesa. During the meeting of the ugly Marquesa and the beautiful actress, the talk is mainly of Dona Clara, the Marquesa's only concern. A few years before, the Marquesa had acquired the services of Pepita, an orphan, from the Abbess Madre Maria del Pilar. The kind and talented old nun planned that Pepita would one day take over her position as head of the religious order, and she saw in this opportunity for the young girl to be the Marquesa's companion a fine apprenticeship in the ways of the world. But Pepita is quite unhappy, for she sees the Marquesa at her worst - an ugly, selfish, mean and bitter old woman. While on a pilgrimage on behalf of Dona Clara's forthcoming baby, the Marquesa discovers a letter Pepita has written to the Abbess, in which this good girl relates her sad state. At first upset by its contents, the Marquesa resolves to become a better person, especially in her treatment of Pepita. We know from Pepita's letter, however, that her only wish is to return to the convent. Two days later both the Marquesa and Pepita are on the bridge when it falls.

PART III - "ESTEBAN"

The second **episode** tells the story of Esteban and Manuel, twin foundlings left on the doorstep of the convent. The Abbess raised them as her own sons, and when they left the convent they earned their living by doing odd jobs. The brothers were as one and their deep love for one another was obvious even to the casual spectator. Physically, they appear to the reader as identical and in their youth they had developed a language only understood by themselves. At first they earn their livings as scribes, but soon go on to more adventurous activities on the docks and about the countryside. When they return to Lima and once again earn their living as scribes, Manuel falls deeply in love with La Perichole. It is ironic that love of another should come between the exemplary love of these brothers. Manuel attempts to hide his new love, but screams it out one night in a delirium caused by an infection he has in his leg. Nevertheless, he is willing to abandon his love of the actress for love of his brother. Manuel dies of the infection and Esteban wanders alone and detached from the world. His abyss of loneliness is so great that he attempts suicide but is saved by Captain Alvarado, the explorer, with whom he agrees to sail around the world. The captain, who seems to be a kindred spirit, has also suffered a great loss in the death of a daughter whom he loved very much. He tells Esteban that life is too short to commit suicide. On their way to begin the voyage the next day, Esteban crosses the Bridge of San Luis Rey while Captain Alvarado descends with the baggage to cross the stream by raft. Esteban falls to his death with the four other travelers.

PART IV - "UNCLE PIO"

The third **episode**, which constitutes the final part of the body of the novel, tells the story of Uncle Pio, Camila Perichole, the Viceroy, the Archbishop, and Jaime, La Perichole's illegitimate son. Uncle Pio has had a varied and adventurous career, first in Spain and later in Peru. Many of his enterprises border on the illegal, but for the most part he is a charming opportunist who knows and has some dealings with everyone from the Viceroy to the least important peasant. He is a lover of the arts, especially music, and he has written some folk music which is known to this day. He discovered Camila Perichole at the age of twelve when she was singing in a cheap cafe. He guides her career for the next several years until she becomes the greatest actress in all Peru. Uncle Pio's name describes his relationship to everyone - he is their "uncle." But his relationship with La Perichole transcends this and he falls deeply in love with her. However, once she becomes famous, she spurns him and becomes the mistress of the Viceroy. She also bears the Viceroy three children.

La Perichole's career is hurt by the scandal of the Viceroy and their children, and she retires from the stage to concentrate on gaining a social position. Later she looses her beauty when her face is permanently scared by smallpox. Despite these moral and physical blemishes, Uncle Pio still loves her. But she still spurns his love and lives a secluded and bitter life. She agrees to give her son Jaime, a sickly child, to Uncle Pio to raise in the tradition of an aristocrat. In the last part of the story she is contrite as she realizes her own pride has made her unable to love those who loved her.

PART V - "PERHAPS AN INTENTION"

In the last part of the novel, we return to the theological surmises of Brother Juniper. We learn that his case history of the bridge incident is not the first attempt that Brother Juniper has made at finding a logical and scientific rationale to explain faith and the workings of God. Once when a village was struck by a pestilence, he tried to analyze the goodness, piety, and usefulness of each villager to determine if there was a logical reason for the pestilence striking there specifically. His only conclusion was that the good people suffered more than the bad ones. His faith somewhat shattered, he quickly destroyed his findings. In this instance, however, he decides to push his inquiry about the victims of the bridge. He interviews the Abbess, Captain Alvarado, and La Perichole. He soon discovers that he gains better facts from people who were not closely connected or emotionally involved with the victims. His only conclusion is the conjecture that the wicked are killed and the good die young. While he is not satisfied with his findings, the Church authorities are satisfied enough by his study to burn him as a heretic.

The Archbishop, the Viceroy, the Abbess, and Captain Alvarado are all present at the execution. La Perichole does not attend, and her depression is intensified when she learns that the Viceroy is sending their two daughters to a convent school in Spain. Miserable and alone, La Perichole seeks out the Abbess to gain some comfort from this pious lady who also suffered a personal loss in the fall of the bridge. Sitting in the garden of the convent, La Perichole pours out all the despair of her lifetime.

In the last scene of the story, Dona Clara, the Marquesa's daughter, also visits the Abbess and shows her the last letter she received from her mother. This is the letter in which the

Marquesa renounced the pettiness and selfishness of her past life and resolved to lead a better life and to treat Pepita with the utmost civility and kindness. The Abbess interprets the letter as an example of God's grace, and the Condesa sees her mother as she never saw her before. In a final soliloquy, the Abbess reflects on her love for Pepita and Esteban, on Camila's love for Uncle Pio and Jaime, and on Dona Clara's new found love for her mother. She fears that when she and Perichole and Dona Clara die no one will remember the others. But this does not really matter because they were loved - and love is the only meaningful thing in life.

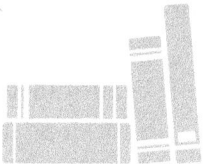

THE BRIDGE OF SAN LUIS REY

CHARACTER ANALYSES

DONA MARIA, MARQUESA DE MONTEMAYOR

The Marquesa is the daughter of a prosperous textile merchant. Her youth is influenced by her ugliness, stuttering, and constant friction with her parents. She is lonely and bitter, and at twenty-six she marries a nondescript nobleman. They have one child, Dona Clara, upon whom Dona Maria heaps all the affection-starved shortcomings of her own life. To use a popular phrase Dona Clara is not mothered, she is "smothered." Her mother adores the girl but soon Dona Clara revolts by marrying Conde Vicente d'Abuirre and leaving Peru and her mother to take up residence at the Spanish Court. The Marquesa becomes more lonely and miserable. Her wealth gives her little comfort and she slowly loses her faith, takes to drinking quite regularly, and becomes a malicious gossip. An attempt at reconciliation between the mother and daughter takes place four years after Dona Clara's marriage, when the pathetic Marquesa visits Spain, but Dona Clara's pride and Dona Maria's pomposity forbid a joyous reunion. Henceforth, the relationship is carried out only in letters.

But even filling these beautiful letters with the endless details of daily life and society does not abate the miserable loneliness of this aging woman. She talks about her daughter to whoever will listen. Pepita, the protege of the Abbess from the convent, comes to live with the Marquesa as her companion. The young girl suffers greatly as she tries her best to help the ugly, selfish, and miserable old lady. When Pepita writes the Abbess of her unhappiness, the Marquesa reads the letter. It creates a reaction as the Marquesa sees herself for the first time as she really is. She resolves to change, especially in her treatment of her young companion, but she dies two days later when the bridge falls.

PEPITA

An orphan girl, she is raised and greatly loved by the Abbess. The Abbess, who dreams of making Pepita her successor, allows the young girl to become the Marquesa's companion in order to gain some worldly experience at the court. But as a pious child, she suffers greatly in her new position. She is hated by her fellow servants because she does not steal or take advantage of the Marquesa; she is embarrassed when the Marquesa parades through the streets and the young girl's modesty and virtue are exposed to the eyes of worldly men and boys; but most of all, she cannot understand the erratic and demented behavior of her mistress. Pepita suffers all these things as an act of obedience to the Abbess. Like all true obedience, hers is an act of love for the Abbess. Finally, in desperation, she writes the letter describing her unhappiness. When the Marquesa reads that letter and confronts her with it, the young child merely replies that it was not a courageous thing to have done. A model of the pious, humble, and charitable life, Pepita dies with her mistress when the bridge falls.

DONA CLARA (CONDESA D'ABUIRRE)

Daughter of the Marquesa, she is nearly the opposite of her mother in temperament and physical attributes. She is vain, political, and intellectual. At the Spanish Court she is known as a patroness of the arts and sciences. Even after marriage she continues to bicker with her mother over money matters. She enjoys her mother's detailed letters, but cannot tolerate her presence. In an interview with the Abbess at the end of the story, she is quite defensive about her mother, but both she and the Abbess share in the joy of the Marquesa's last letter, in which she resolved to change her ways.

THE ABBESS MADRE MARIA DEL PILAR

This kind, shrewd, idealistic, yet practical old Abbess is the only character in the story who knows all the other characters. She has raised Pepita, Esteban, and Manuel, and she sends Pepita to the Marquesa as a companion; she knows the Viceroy and Uncle Pio, and, of course, the Archbishop; she is interviewed by Brother Juniper when he is assembling his case; and, finally, Perichole, Dona Clara, and the Abbess share a common grief over a personal loss in the tragedy of the bridge. The narrator tells us that the Abbess and the Marquesa are remembered as the greatest women of the times, the former for her charitable works and the latter for her letters. Described as a financial and political genius for the orphanages, schools, hospitals, and convents which she has been able to build she is nevertheless a woman of great warmth and virtue. She raises Pepita, Esteban, and Manuel as her own children, and it is only her faith and belief in the meaningfulness of love which allows her to continue her great work after her three loved ones die.

UNCLE PIO

The illegitimate child of a fine Castilian family, in Spain, he ran away from home to Madrid. He has always led the life of an adventurer and has the qualities necessary for such a life. He is intelligent, multilingual, talented at disguises, good at remembering names, a master at conversation, highly secretive in his activities, and possesses a flexible morality. By the time he reaches manhood he has three goals in life: first, he loves independence; second, he desires to be in the company of beautiful women; and third, he wants to have a part, however small, in Spanish literature, especially the theater. After a barroom quarrel, he migrates to Peru, where he occupies himself at various trades, composes folk music, knows and becomes known by everyone. He discovers, trains, and manages the career of La Perichole, transforming her into a great actress. He loves her deeply, but always from a distance. He sees her decline first through her immoral relationship with the Viceroy, later during her withdrawal from the theater, and finally with the smallpox which destroys her beauty. Uncle Pio forces Perichole to see him and requests that she allow him to raise Jaime. Perhaps out of love, more likely out of despair, she consents, and Uncle Pio and Jaime set out to begin a new life. However, both die when the bridge falls.

BROTHER JUNIPER

A philosophical Franciscan monk, Brother Juniper has worked successfully in the mission field of Peru for several years. He witnessed the fall of the bridge. In an attempt to show scientifically the accident as part of God's scheme in the universe, he investigates the lives of the victims. But his conclusions do little to advance the philosophical question of whether men live by design or accident. He is burned as a heretic, and the original copy of his study is burned with him. The three middle **episodes** of the novel are based on a second copy of his study which was discovered by the narrator. Brother Juniper maintains his faith in spite of his findings in this case and in lesser scientific studies he has made in attempts to prove his theology. He even sees his own execution as part of God's will.

THE VICEROY OF PERU (DON ANDRES DE RIBERA)

A widower, soldier, and former member of the Spanish diplomatic delegations in Rome and in Versailles, he is unhappy with his current office. A proud and sickly man, he symbolizes the idle rich and the worst of colonial government. Camila Perichole becomes his mistress and they have three children -Jaime, a boy, and two girls, whom the Viceroy sends to a convent school in Spain. When Perichole becomes ill with smallpox and secludes herself in her villa, she refuses to see him and she returns many of his gifts and writes him a bitter letter, ending their affair.

JAIME

The illegitimate son of Camila Perichole and the Viceroy, the young boy is plagued by his father's poor health and endowed with his mother's extraordinary beauty. Perichole entrusts his upbringing to Uncle Pio, but both die when the bridge falls.

CONDE VICENTE D'ABUIRRE

He is Dona Clara's husband and a fairly important person at the Spanish Court.

JENARITO

He is a servant of the Marquesa.

THE ARCHBISHOP

A fat, self-satisfied man, he is epicurean in his diet, but otherwise leads an exemplary life to compensate for his eating habits. He is a friend of the Viceroy's, an admirer of La Perichole, and a detractor of the Abbess. He views the ideals of Rome and theology as very remote from the primitive Church of Peru. Idle and disinterested in his duties but a slave to the pomp of his office, he looks forward to the day he can retire to his villa in Italy.

CAPTAIN ALVARADO

An explorer, adventurer, and ship's captain, he is friend of the Marquesa and the Abbess. He knows the depths of grief, because several years before he lost his own daughter, a beautiful child whom he deeply loved. The Captain saves Esteban from committing suicide and convinces him to live out his days because life is so short anyway. He and Esteban plan to sail together, but Esteban falls to his death when the bridge collapses. The Captain is in the gorge below supervising the baggage. Later the Captain views with disdain the execution of Brother Juniper.

CAMILA PERICHOLE

La Perichole's real name is Micaela Villegas and she is earning her living singing in cafes when Uncle Pio discovers her at the age of twelve. Her story is the stereotyped "rags to riches to rags" cycle. Uncle Pio takes her raw and awkward talent, and together with his knowledge and patience and their combined dedication to work, changes her into "La Perichole," the greatest actress in the Spanish world. At the height of her career, Camila becomes the mistress of the Viceroy, to whom she bears three children before discovering that she does not really love him. Camila has long desired status among the small aristocracy of Peru. Retiring from the stage, she devotes five years to this futile project. Through all this, the patient and loving Uncle Pio sits sadly in the wings very much like Cyrano de Bergerac. When Uncle Pio visits her at her country villa, she insists on being called Dona Micaela, and she quickly dismisses his suggestion that she return to the stage as steadfastly as she rejects his love.

When Dona Micaela's beauty is destroyed by smallpox, she lives in complete seclusion. The Viceroy sends a heartbreaking message that he is sending their two daughters to Spain. Her life shattered, her income unstable, Camila is bitter and disillusioned. She agrees to allow Uncle Pio to raise Jaime in an aristocrat manner. When the bridge falls, she looses the only man who ever really loved her and the son she loved so much. In the final scene of the novel she seeks comfort from the Abbess to ease her sad and guilt-ridden final days. Loved by so many, it is ironic that this woman was never able to love.

ESTEBAN AND MANUEL

Twin brothers, these foundlings are raised by the Abbess. When they are too old to remain at the convent they depart to make their way in the world. Earning their living chiefly as scribes, they are inseparable in mind and spirit. Manuel falls in love with La Perichole but sacrifices this love when he sees it will separate the two brothers. Manuel dies of an infection and Esteban enters a long period of grief which culminates in an attempted suicide. Captain Alvarado's belief that life is too short to end it by suicide seems to restore Esteban's sense of reality. He plans to sail with the Captain in hope of finding a new meaning to life when he dies in the accident of the bridge.

Comment

Despite the philosophical and theological overtones of the novel, *The Bridge of San Luis Rey* is not primarily a philosophical or theological work. Brother Juniper's thesis provides the motivation for an insight into and a delineation of several interesting characters in the Peru of two centuries ago. Like Brother Juniper, our conclusion as to whether we live by accident or design can only be a conjecture and generalization.

The success of the story is due to its excellent characterizations. The best portrait is probably the romantic figure of Uncle Pio, who has so many gifts yet must go through life always loving from a distance. The second most interesting character is the Abbess - a dedicated servant of God yet possessing all the political awareness which the Archbishop of the story lacks. Pepita, Esteban, and Manuel are fitting extensions of the Abbess personality. The two most tragic figures in the story are the Marquesa and La Perichole. Both desiring the other's way of life, they lack the insight to know that they would still be unhappy with it and that the quality they really lack is an ability to love. What basic human need do all the characters seek? The answer is the **theme** of the book - namely, love, the principal ingredient of the good life.

The Marquesa's personality has developed in its way because of a lack of love in her childhood, and while the motivation of her letters is ostensibly the love of her daughter, she still is not happy. Her great transformation will include acceptance and love of Pepita. Uncle Pio will indirectly continue his love of Perichole by raising Jaime. Perichole's basic sorrow is that she does know how to love. Love of the Abbess brings Pepita her only joy and it adds greatly to the happiness of Manuel and Esteban. The Viceroy, who seems to have everything a man could desire, is not really happy until he loves Camila. Even Brother Juniper's investigation is begun, carried on, and concluded out of his love of God.

If we accept the **theme**, symbolism and **imagery** of the novel, life and death are facts, but the bridge which spans the two is love - love which gives life its truest meaning and love which survives us when we die.

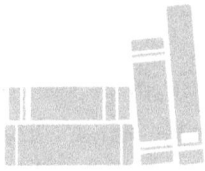

THE BRIDGE OF SAN LUIS REY

ESSAY QUESTIONS AND ANSWERS

Question: What is the function of the Abbess?

Answer: The Abbess acts as a unifying element in the novel. She is the only character who knows all the other characters and she appears in all the episodes. As the Abbess of the orphanage, she raises Pepita, Manuel, and Esteban, all of whom are foundlings. A common religion brings her in contact with the Archbishop; a common concern about people associates her with the Viceroy; and her need of money for her charities leads her to befriend the Marquesa and loan her Pepita as a companion. She sensitively follows the careers, joys and hopes of Manuel and Esteban, whom she has raised as sons. It is she who sends Captain Alvarado to help Esteban when he is depressed over the death of his brother. At the end of the novel, Camila Perichole, formerly a great actress, and Dona Clara, the daughter of the Marquesa, share their grief with the strong nun who also suffered a personal loss when the bridge fell. The Abbess' secure faith and belief that the important thing in life is to love someone lessens the guilt of the two younger women. The Abbess is the epitome of man's love for his fellow human beings; she has dedicated her life to humanity, and perhaps like the "saints and poets" alluded to in *Our Town,* she appreciates every precious experience of life.

Question: What is the structure of the novel?

Answer: *The Bridge of San Luis Rey* is divided into five parts. The first and last are comparable to a prologue and an epilogue. In the first part we are told by a narrator of the collapse of the bridge and the death of five travelers. We are also introduced to the inquisitive Brother Juniper, who witnesses the accident and proposes to investigate the lives of these travelers to show that their deaths were a logical step in God's scheme of the universe. In the last part of the novel we learn that Brother Juniper's study has been futile and he has been put to death for his skepticism. Symbolically, we can interpret this as meaning that man should never be so bold as to question God's plan. But we can certainly conclude that neither Brother Juniper nor the narrator resolves the problem of whether man lives by chance or design, and it still remains a philosophical riddle. The three middle parts of the story are based on materials which the narrator found in an old copy of Brother Juniper's manuscript. An episodic structure dominates the three middle parts of the novel, which are detailed characterizations of the five victims of the bridge and their friends. Their lives are ironically interwoven by time, location, and circumstance. They all contribute to the **theme** of the novel because they are motivated by love or by lack of it. We learn in the first part of the story that Brother Juniper's study took about six years to compile, but in the three core chapters the characters are chronologically developed from their childhoods to their deaths on the bridge.

Question: At what point in their lives did each of the characters die?

Answer: Brother Juniper's study showed that each of the major characters in the study was at a turning point in his life. The Marquesa had recently been given a new insight into herself when she read Pepita's unhappy letter. She had resolved to rededicate her life to humility and charity. Pepita who loved the Abbess more than anyone in the world had decided not to write her letter and chose to continue her self-sacrificing life as the Marquesa's companion. Esteban had slowly begun to recover from the loss of Manuel, the twin brother he loved so dearly, and he was ready to begin a new life of adventure with Captain Alvarado, the explorer. Uncle Pio, who has long loved Camila, finally convinces her to allow him to raise her son Jaime. In this way, Uncle Pio symbolically continues his love of Camila, still from a distance. Even Jaime, sickly and illegitimate, was now given a new lease on life, for he would be brought up by the same kindly man who had raised and taught his mother so many things. But the bridge falls, killing each of these travelers before they begin their new lives. Perhaps their lives were now whole or complete because they had all learned to live with their problems. Like Brother Juniper and the narrator, perhaps it is not for us to know.

Question: What was the effect of the accident on the living?

Answer: For most Peruvians who did not have a personal loss when the bridge fell, the accident was an occasion for thanking God that it did not fall when they were on it. Of course, the accident motivated Brother Juniper's study. Captain Alvarado, the Archbishop, and the Viceroy show the isolation of command, and go about their business in a stoical manner. The three people who are most affected are the Abbess, the Condesa, and Camila. The Abbess lost Pepita, the young girl she had secretly hoped would one day succeed her. She also lost Esteban who was like a son to her. The Condesa lost her mother, and although they had bickered and even hated each other for many years, she learned of her mother's desire to change her ways from the Marquesa's last letter. Camila Perichole lost her beloved son Jaime and the only man who had truly loved her and who she regretfully tells us she was not able to love. After consoling the other two women at the end of the novel, the Abbess makes her philosophical statement that death is secondary to the fact that the victims are loved, and love is the only meaning and only survival in life.

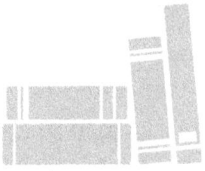

HEAVEN'S MY DESTINATION

INTRODUCTION

After the successful reception of *The Bridge of San Luis Rey*, Wilder left his teaching position at Lawrenceville and traveled in Europe studying continental drama. The following year, 1930, he published *The Woman of Andros,* a fable set in pre-Christian Greece. While the novel is highly regarded by some contemporary critics, it was for the most part unpopular with the critics and public of the early 1930s. There is an underlying thought in the story that if the characters had lived in Christian times, their lives would have been happier. The decade of 1930-1940 was to be the most prolific in Thornton Wilder's career. Besides *The Woman of Andros* in 1930, he published *The Long Christmas Dinner and Other Plays,* a collection of one-act plays, including *Pullman Car Hiawatha,* in 1931; a translation and adaptation of Andre Obey's *Lucrece* for the American stage, in 1933; *Heaven's My Destination,* in 1935; *Our Town* in 1938; and *The Merchant of Yonkers* in the same year. This play was later revised and renamed *The Matchmaker.*

Whereas his three previous novels had foreign settings (*The Cabala* in Rome, *The Bridge of San Luis Rey* in Peru, and *The Woman of Andros* in Greece), *Heaven's My Destination* is set in the midwestern United States in the early thirties. It may be termed Wilder's most orthodox novel - that is, it follows those requirements for action and character development which we usually associate with the popular novel. Its publication marked Wilder's last novel for nearly thirteen years until the publication of *The Ides of March* in 1948. Between these novels Wilder taught at the University of Chicago, lectured widely, and most importantly, devoted his creative efforts to the theater. The result of these efforts at drama were *Our Town* (1938), which we have already discussed, *The Skin of Our Teeth* (1942), and *The Matchmaker*, both of which we shall discuss later.

However, there are certain dramatic techniques used in *Heaven's My Destination*. For example, the chapter titles are actually stage instructions which introduce the characters, set the scene, and contribute to moving the action. A similar technique is seen in *Moby Dick*, where Melville borrows Shakespearean stage directions for many of the novel's chapter titles. While the characterization in this novel is not as precise as that in *The Cabala* or *The Bridge of San Luis Rey*, elements of **satire** and **irony** are more evident. In this novel Wilder satirizes everything he was nearly to deify a few years later in *Our Town*. The good life, marriage, politics, banking, business, and many other aspects of modern life each receive their respective jibes. In point of time, the action covers a year in the life of George Brush, a traveling book salesman. His territory is the midwestern United States, so we follow him back and forth across the corn belt and the evangelical belt. The structure of the story is episodic and the only detailed characterization is of George. His tragedy is his failure to change - to mature from the various experiences he has. At the end of the novel we find him in exactly the same town where the story begins. Sadly, he has only a little more insight than he did the year before, although he has had a myriad of varied adventures in his travels.

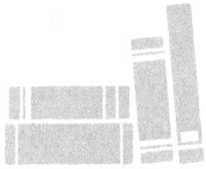

HEAVEN'S MY DESTINATION

PLOT ANALYSIS

George Brush is a traveling textbook salesman in the midwestern United States. Unlike the stereotyped, joke-telling, and promiscuous salesman familiar in much fiction, George is intensely and sincerely religious. He feels compelled to write Biblical quotations on hotel desk blotters, destroy suggestive pictures on the front of movie houses, and kneel beside his Pullman car berth when saying his evening prayers. He is a non-smoker and a non-gambler. Besides avoiding these vices, he feels that it is necessary to help his fellow man lead a virtuous life also. All his conversations have an evangelical bent. He refers to strangers as brothers and sisters, and turns the other cheek whenever trouble arises. As might be expected, most people resent George's interference in their personal lives.

In Wellington, Oklahoma, on his twenty-third birthday, George is confronted by Doremus Blodgett, a hosiery salesman. A worldly man, Blodgett questions George on his evangelical activities, and when he asks George why he isn't a minister, George replies that he isn't fit to be since he once got a girl in trouble. George is willing to face the consequences but he cannot find the girl. Blodgett, who is traveling with a woman he calls his "cousin," invites George to a rendezvous the following evening at the McGraw House in Oklahoma City.

Meanwhile George goes to Arminia to withdraw his savings from the local bank. He refuses to accept the interest because he feels that interest is immoral. Insulted, Timothy Southwick, the bank president, has George arrested and run out of town. Ironically, the whole ridiculous incident causes a run on the bank. The police as well as the bank personnel think George is insane.

The following evening, George has an uncomfortable visit with Blodgett and his companion during which he reveals that he is a graduate of Shiloh Baptist College in South Dakota, and that his goal in life is to settle down to a good American family life and have six children. Blodgett's companion, Mrs. McCoy, forces a drink on George and he babbles out the story of his affair with a farmer's daughter near Kansas City. As far as George is concerned he is married to the girl, whose name he thinks is Roberta. Although he has tried since, he has been unable to locate her or her family. George leaves the hotel room feeling sorry for these worldly drinkers and smokers, and, in their turn, Blodgett and Mrs. McCoy feel George is insane. In response to a telegram from his employer, George visits Judge Corey at a resort called Camp Morgan. The Judge is a powerful member of the educational committee which selects textbooks for the state school system. One of George's tentmates is Dick Roberts, an insurance man who is plagued by nightmares and seems suicidal. George makes his contact with the Judge, who is a slippery and syrupy politician. The Judge introduces George to his daughter, Mississippi, and his wife. Mississippi smokes, drinks, and is morally weak according to George's standards. George sums up the ideal as one who never laughs loudly, never smokes or drinks, but is simple in her ways and morally above reproach. The liberal Mississippi laughs in his face. Later George becomes popular with the campers when he sings a few hymns.

The following day George thinks he finds a kindred moral spirit in Jessie Mayhew, but he quickly rejects her when he learns she believes in evolution. During the night Dick Roberts has one of his nightmares and leads the charitable George on a wild chase which includes the overturning of a canoe which nearly drowns the good samaritan. Later George enlists the help of Judge Corey and his poker circle to drive him after Roberts. George stops the demented insurance man from jumping off a tower and he stays with him all night in the woods. Before George leaves the camp, the judge offers him $35,000 and a nice political position if he will marry Mississippi. George declines but does get the Judge's promise to support his textbooks.

In Kansas City, George shares an apartment with four friends at Miss Craven's boarding house, more familiarly called "Queenies." Over the years this has come to be George's home away from home. He shares the apartment with Herb and Morrie, two newspaper reporters, Bat, a motion-picture technician, and Louis, a chemist turned hospital orderly. George's understanding with his four friends, who are a free living group for the most part, is that he won't preach at them, if they don't sin in front of him. On the night of his return, his roommates get George drunk as a practical joke. He thinks they are giving him medicine for a cold. George, who seems to like his first real taste of liquor, goes out on the town and has a bad hangover the next day.

The following Sunday, George is again fooled by his roommates when they take him to dinner at Ma Crofut's, a house of ill repute. George thinks that all the girls are really Ma Crofut's daughters and the occasion is just a pleasant Sunday dinner in a typical American home. Impressed by their beauty and quiet manners, George invites all the girls to the movies. Returning to Queenie's, George is chided by his three friends, and in the fight which ensues George is hospitalized after he is thrown down the stairs. Queenie visits George in the hospital and tells him that Father Pasziewski is feeling better. Father Pasziewski is Queenie's parish priest, and although he and George have never met, they have become good friends through Queenie.

Later, George asks Louis what he can do to become more popular. Louie tells him to stop being so pious and expecting everyone else to be moral also. George has an hysterical outburst in which he screams, "the whole world is crazy."

When George is well, he again sets out on his rounds between Kansas City and Abilene, Texas. Of all his adventures we are told three. First, George out-preaches the Rev. James Bigelow, an evangelical minister he meets on the train. Second, he visits Mrs. McManus, a medium in Fort Worth. He desires to communicate with Dwight L. Moody, the great evangelist, but before the night is over he exposes Mrs. McManus as a fraud and departs disillusioned by her lies. His third adventure takes place in Pekin, Arkansas. While accompanying Louise Gregg and Miss Simmons to a church social, three rowdies insult Miss Simmons. George hits one of them and forces him to apologize. Hailed as a gentleman and a hero by Mrs. Forrest, the minister, George says in a sermon that the violence was un-Christian and he is not fit to be in the house of the Lord.

Finally George finds the farmer's daughter he had sought for so long. Her name is Roberta Weyerhauser and she is working as a waitress in a Chinese restaurant in Kansas City. After a frustrating attempt at reconciliation, Roberta flatly rejects George's proposal of marriage and even his offers of money and help. While he is visiting his old friend Queenie, George visits his former roommate, Herb, who is dying. Herb asks George to take care of his child and his mother. Depressed, George arranges to care for Herb's mother and brings Herb's four-year-old daughter Elizabeth to live with Queenie. George loses no time in introducing the young girl to the values of scripture.

While on a trip to Clarksville, Missouri, George's charity toward a little girl who is being punished and a man who is robbing a store ends in his own arrest for kidnapping and robbery. In jail George meets George Burkin, an unemployed motion-picture director from New York who has been arrested as a peeping Tom. At the trial George tells of his two previous arrests - one when he sat in a Jim Crow car because he believes in the equality of the races and the other in Arminia because of his feelings about banks. Judge Darwin Carberry recognizes George's nonconformity immediately and calls his wife to come and see the unusual proceedings. In a merry-go-round trial George relates his theories of religion, social progress, Ghandi, etc. He finds a kindred spirit in the Judge, and both he and George Burkin are released. The Judge's final advice to George is to take it easy on the world because there are many people who resent ideas.

On the return trip to Kansas City, the two men pick up a hitchhiker who turns out to be the real robber George had set free a few days before; it quickly becomes evident that the criminal does not want to be converted by George. In a long conversation, George relates for the first time the reason he became so religious. He was converted by Marion Truby at a revival meeting during his sophomore year in college. In addition to that religious conversion George has been strongly influenced by the philosophy of Mahatma Ghandi. Even when George discovered that the woman evangelist was a dope addict, he could not be disillusioned. Burkin is clever enough to realize that George's problem is a closed mind, and the Easterner slowly begins to build a logical case for agnosticism and scepticism. But George's faith will not be lessened.

When George returns to Kansas City he meets Roberta and her sister, Lottie. Lottie convinces Roberta to marry George even though he is crazy - because he is crazy in a nice sort of way. George and Roberta adopt Elizabeth and settle down to what George expects to be a happy American home. Jealous of Elizabeth, lonely because of George's traveling, and because she is incompatible with him. Roberta tells George she wants a divorce and wants to go back to the farm. The strain is too much for George and for the first time in his lifetime he begins to smoke. This is the first sign of the complete mental and physical collapse he suffers while traveling in Texas.

In the hospital, George is visited by a minister and he confesses that he has broken all the Commandments except two - he has never killed anyone nor has he ever adored false idols. George experiences a thrill, when at the height of his illness, he insults the minister and proclaims his atheism, his hate of morality, and his complete distrust of ministers.

While he is in the hospital, George receives a silver spoon and a letter from Queenie. The spoon is a gift from Father Pasziewski, the friend he has never met and who left George the spoon as a gesture of faith as the old priest was dying. Slowly George recovers and returns to selling textbooks in the same territory. Little wiser for all his experiences, he manages to return to Wellington, Oklahoma, where he celebrates his twenty-fourth birthday. It has been a busy year.

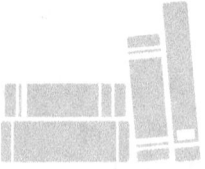

HEAVEN'S MY DESTINATION

CHARACTER ANALYSES

GEORGE BRUSH

George is the main character in the story. He has little insight into his own personality and approaches life with naive innocence. He constantly tells people that he did not go through a great religious experience and dedicate his life to goodness for any insignificant reason. As a result of his friendly and outgoing salesman's personality, he is constantly pushing his beliefs into the lives of other people. In many ways he is selfish and intolerant. He admires Gandhi, practices pacificism, and tries to lead the perfect moral life. For most of the story, George tries to achieve perfection; only at the end of the novel does he realize that he can't be perfect. This vain goal is quite costly. He loses his friends, his wife, and even his mind for a time.

George practices "ahimsa," a Buddhist theory of acting opposite to what is expected. This practice is the basis of his pacifism. It also explains why he allows a thief to go free when he should arrest him. George's chief faults are his smug self-righteousness and his closed mind. His chief attributes are his love and charity toward his fellow man.

DOREMUS BLODGETT

A typical traveling salesman who is loud and worldly, "Reme" baits George for his evangelicism.

MRS. MARGIE MCCOY

Blodgett's traveling "companion."

MR. GIBBS

Manager of the hotel in Wellington, Oklahoma.

MR. TIMOTHY SOUTHWICK

President of the Arminia Savings Bank.

MR. GOGARTY

The Constable in Arminia.

JERRY BOHARDUS

A retired policeman in Arminia.

MRS. COWLES

A housewife in Arminia.

MR. HOWELLS

Salesmanager of Caulkins Educational Press and George's boss.

MRS. CAULKINS

A writer of textbooks and owner of the publishing company George represents.

JUDGE LEONIDAS COREY

A part owner of Camp Morgan, a resort, and a member of the textbook committee which decides which books will be used in the state of Oklahoma.

MISSISSIPPI

His daughter.

DICK ROBERTS

A mentally ill vacationer at Camp Morgan who suffers from nightmares. George saves him from suicide.

GEORGE ROBERTS

His son.

MR. MACKLIN

The nature counselor at Camp Morgan.

JESSIE MAYHEW

A girl at Camp Morgan. George is attracted to her until he discovers she believes in evolution.

JUDGE COREY'S POKER CIRCLE.

Helma, Solario, Jeannie Socket, Bill Watkins, Mike Kusack

MISS CRAVEN

Better known as Queenie, she operates the boarding house in Kansas City where George stays.

BOARDERS AT MISS CRAVEN'S.

Mr. Morris, Mr. Callahan

FATHER PASZIEWSKI

Miss Craven's parish priest, he is pious and sickly. Although they never meet, he and George become good friends through Miss Craven.

MEMBERS OF THE ST. VERONICA GUILD WHO CARE FOR FATHER PASZIEWSKI.

Mrs. Kramer, Mrs. Delehanty, Mrs. Kandinsky

GEORGE'S ROOMMATES AT QUEENIE'S.

Herb, A newspaperman; Morrie, A newspaperman; Louie, A hospital orderly; Bat, A motion picture technician

ELIZABETH

Herb's daughter.

MRS. CROFUT

A Madam.

MRS. CROFUT'S "DAUGHTERS."

Lily Dolores, May, Ruth, Mayme, Gladys

JIMMY

A policeman in Kansas City.

MRS. KUBINSKY

A friend and neighbor of Miss Cramer's, she runs a rooming house next door. George takes a room there after his roommates beat him up.

REV. JAMES BIGELOW

An evangelist George meets on the train to Texas.

FRIENDS OF GEORGE'S IN PEKIN, ARKANSAS.

Louise, Greggs, Miss Simmons

THE BOYS WHO INSULT MISS SIMMONS.

Bill, Fred, Javis, Cronin

MR. FORREST

The minister in Pekin, Arkansas.

MISS ROBERTA WEYERHAUSER

The girl George wrongs and later marries to assuage his guilt. She is very unhappy in the marriage and leaves George to return to the farm.

LOTTIE

Her sister.

MR. BAKER

Owner of the hotel in Clarksville, Missouri.

THE GRUBERS

The parents of Rhoda May Gruber, the girl George is charged with attempting to kidnap. The case is thrown out of court.

MRS. EFRIM

Owner of the general store which George is accused of robbing.

MRS. ROBINSON

A customer of Mrs. Efrim's.

MR. WARREN

The constable in Clarksville.

GEORGE BURKIN

An unemployed motion-picture director from New York who is arrested as a peeping Tom in Clarksville. He attempts to have George see reality, but George rejects him and his ideas.

JUDGE DARWIN CARBERRY

The philosophical judge who releases Brush and Burkin.

EMMA CARBERRY

His wife.

FRED HART

The mayor of Clarksville.

LUCILE HART

His wife.

HAWKINS

The real robber of Mrs. Efrim's store whom George sets free because of his philosophy of "ahimsa."

MARION TRUBY

The sixteen-year-old evangelist who converted George in his sophomore year in college. Later he discovers she was a dope addict.

DR. BOWIE

The minister who visits George in the hospital.

MISS COLLOQUER

George's nurse.

Comment

In none of his other plays or novels does Thornton Wilder develop a character as fully as he does George Marvin Brush in this work. While on the surface George appears as a religious fanatic, we cannot dismiss him with that label only. Despite his evangelism one cannot help admiring him for his nonconformity, self-reliance, and sincerity. Unlike Sinclair Lewis' *Elmer Gantry,* George is no hypocrite. The only error he made (with Roberta) he is willing to correct by taking care of her for life. His kindness toward Elizabeth, his chivalrous behavior on behalf of old Miss Simmons, and his empathy for the ten-year-old girl who has to wear a sign saying "I AM A LIAR," are all actions which make us admire him.

On the other hand we resent his model life, and his interference in that basic Constitutional right -freedom of religion. Our resentment is first like Blodgett's - motivated by jealousy, but later, like one of George's college professors and George Burkin, we come to see that George is really narrow and petty as a result of his closed mind. Because of this limited view of the world, George experiences little growth. He demands ideals the real world can never attain. Under strain he even breaks his own rules, for example, smoking, but the only time he rebels is when he has his breakdown in Texas. That side of George Brush shows only for a moment however. When he is well, he returns to the same job and even the same town for his birthday. Still he has not profited significantly from a whole year's experience. However, there is a slight glimmer of tolerance and growth at the very end of the story when he helps a girl who believes in evolution.

More than most of Wilder's other works, *Heaven's My Destination* contains some of the most humorous scenes he has written. The trial in Clarksville, George's first arrest, and the scene at Mrs. Crofut's Sunday dinner are among the best.

The main aspects of human nature satirized are man's naivete and many of the social and economic crises of the 1930s. Wilder's **theme** here is that faith is not enough to exist on in a materialistic society like ours. Faith must be supported by reason; it must grow as the personality develops and grows. To quote an old adage: "If you cease to grow, you commence to die."

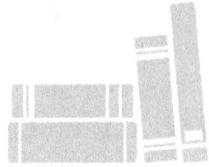

HEAVEN'S MY DESTINATION

ESSAY QUESTIONS AND ANSWERS

Question: What are some of George's unique theories which cause him to get into trouble?

Answer: Probably the two theories which cause George the most trouble are his opinion on banks and his theory of "ahimsa." Early in the story George goes to the Arminia Savings Bank to withdraw his savings. When the teller gives George the interest, he refuses to accept it. Mr. Southwick, a stereotyped bank president, questions George's refusal to accept the interest. George tells him that he has taken a vow of poverty and he usually gives his whole pay check away. He has been feeling guilty over the five hundred dollars he has had on deposit but soon he will give that away also. When George tells Mr. Southwick that having money in the bank is merely an indication of man's insecurity - a symbol of fear - the president quickly has George arrested, and the police chief tells him to leave the town. Of course, they all think George is insane, but his references to a "shaky" bank cause the townspeople to run and withdraw their money. While George was merely applying his ideals in his references to insecurity, the fear of banks closing was a very real one to the people of the 1930s.

George learned about "ahimsa" by studying Gandhi, the great pacifist of India. "Ahimsa" is a theory of pacifism or doing the reverse of what is expected. Henry David Thoreau practiced it when he refused to pay his taxes because of his belief that the Mexican War was morally wrong. In our own time Nobel Peace Prize winner Dr. Martin Luther King practices "ahimsa" in the civil rights movement. But George applies this theory to a ridiculous situation when he tells Hawkins, a man robbing Mrs. Efrim's store in Clarksville, Missouri, to take the money and go free. He says this after he takes Hawkin's gun away. The poor criminal is so confused he doesn't know whether to remain or escape. George's theory is that by doing the opposite of what the criminal expected, the man would come to respect society and reform. As Judge Darwin Carberry tells George after the matter is cleared up - the world just isn't ready for these ideas.

Question: Why does George fail at love and later at marriage?

Answer: George, as he does in most of his relationships in life, sets his goals too high. He wants the perfect woman. According to his standards, this means that she does not smoke, drink, laugh loudly, sin, believe in evolution, etc. George dreams of the perfect American family - Sunday dinners, no illnesses, plenty of laxatives, and six children. George's problem is that he is an idealist and there is no woman on earth who could meet all his specifications; he is also a perfectionist, and no woman could live with his demands. George rejects Mississippi Corey because she drinks and smokes; he rejects Jessie Mayhew because she believes in evolution; finally he marries Roberta, because he feels bound to, even though she is hesitant in the first place. George experiences difficulty in finding things to discuss with Roberta. He takes notes during the day so that he can converse with her in the evenings. Elizabeth, their adopted child, also comes between them since she prefers George. The discrepancy in cultural level between the two grows as their marriage continues; Roberta's major interest is the movies, George desires to read the Encyclopedia Britannica. Finally, George's only thoughts on the purpose of marriage are that it is good for society and it is moral.

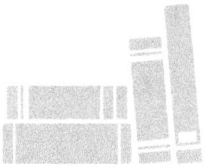

OUR TOWN

INTRODUCTION

Our Town, Thornton Wilder's most popular play, was first performed on January 22, 1938. It was performed at the Henry Miller Theatre in New York City two weeks later and enjoyed a long run. The play has always been a favorite with theatre audiences, and today it is still staged by many school and amateur theatre groups. In a survey of the literature read at present in American high schools, published last year by the Educational Testing Service of Princeton, New Jersey, *Our Town* appears on the reading lists of nearly fifty percent of the schools surveyed. In the next several sections we will discuss many of the features that have made this work so popular with audiences who see it, teachers who have to teach it, and the thousands of students who read it every year, some for the first time, others for the seventh. The inherent goodness, wholesomeness, and optimism of the play have also made it popular with foreign students and audiences.

STRUCTURE AND TIME SEQUENCE

The most unique character in the play is the Stage Manager. As the play opens we immediately notice that there is no curtain and little scenery. A man who is obviously the Stage Manager is arranging what few props are used in Act I. Soon he comes forward and begins an introduction consisting of such details as who wrote the play, who the actors are, and where the action takes place. From this time on, we realize the production will be unique. However, the informality and colloquial language of the Stage Manager keeps us at ease. This use of a narrator as part of the play can probably be traced back to days of Greek drama. The great Greek tragedians employed a chorus in much the same way Wilder uses the Stage Manager. It was the purpose of the chorus to comment on the play between the dialogue of the actors. Initially the chorus had a greater role in Greek tragedies but its role diminished as, at first, one actor, then two, three, etc. were added. In the many centuries between the classical days of Greek drama and today's contemporary productions, there have been several examples of a chorus-like player. When an actor is not in the direct action of the play and comments on the proceedings, he is simulating the role of the chorus. It can be seen occasionally in the plays of Shakespeare when he has a single player recite a prologue or an epilogue. T. S. Eliot and Eugene O'Neil also experimented with a modified chorus technique. Tennessee Williams successfully uses a narrator-technique with his character of "Jim" in *The Glass Menagerie*. While the Stage Manager in *Our Town* never explicitly defines his role, Tennessee Williams' "Jim" tells us very early in the play that he is both the narrator and an actor in the production. In Wilder's play, the Stage Manager also assumes the roles of a woman in the street, the druggist, and the minister who marries George and Emily.

Our Town is divided into the usual three acts, and the Stage Manager opens each act with some introductory remarks and some insight into the future. He is also the last character to speak in each act. His final remarks at the conclusions of Acts I and II are brief, but at the end of Act III he rambles on for a while in order to return the mood to the same informality with which he opened the play.

The action spans thirteen years, from 1901 to 1913. Act I is called "Daily Life" and takes place on May 7, 1901, a typical day in the life of a small New England town. Act II is called "Love and Marriage" and most of the action takes place on July 7, 1904, the day of George and Emily's wedding. However, there is one flashback scene in this act which takes us back to the sensitive scene of the day that George and Emily decide to spend the rest of their lives together. Act III takes place on a summer day in 1913. The title of this act is only hinted, but we can easily guess what it is since most of the action concerns Emily's funeral and the conversations among the dead in the cemetery. In this act also, there is a flashback scene to February 11, 1899, the date of Emily's twelfth birthday.

There is a parallel development of action in Acts I and II. The dialogue switches quickly from the scenes in the kitchen of the Gibbs' home to a similar scene in the kitchen of the Webb household. The two principal scenes played in this parallel manner are the introductory breakfast scene and the trying emotional scenes in each home on the morning of the wedding.

SCENERY AND PROPERTY

Applying his belief that the basis of good drama is a set of pretenses, Wilder uses this air of makebelieve to a high degree in *Our Town*. When the audience enters, it finds a bare stage and no curtain. This device helps Wilder to achieve part of his artistic credo - that the drama could be taking place in any town at any time in early twentieth century America. The stage is in half light, and as the audience enters the stage manager places a table and three chairs on the left hand side of the stage and another table and three chairs on the right side of the stage. He also arranges a bench which will represent the corner of the Webb home. Two flower-covered trellises represent the backyards of the adjacent Gibb and Webb homes.

By gestures and verbal description the Stage Manager creates an imaginary New England town. Beginning with Main Street, his oral architecture creates images of the mountains and hills which border the town, the railroad station, the churches of the Congregational, Presbyterian, Methodist, Unitarian, Baptist, and Catholic denominations. Across the tracks, where the Catholic church is located, there is also a Polish neighborhood and a few French Canadian families. The town hall, post office, and jail are all in the same building. The Stage Manager suggests that Mrs. Gibbs' flowers are sufficient scenery for those who need it. He then describes the cemetery, some of whose gravestones go back to the late 17th century. A train whistle announces the arrival of the 5:45 train for Boston.

Many of the conventional props of the characters are imaginary. Mrs. Gibbs raises an imaginary kitchen shade, Dr. Gibbs puts down an imaginary black bag. Mrs. Webb goes through the imaginary motion of putting wood in the stove, lighting it, and preparing breakfast. Dr. Gibbs reads an imaginary newspaper.

Actual props are held to a minimum: an apron for Mrs. Webb, a hat and handkerchief for Dr. Gibbs, and strapped books for the school children. The sound of rattling milk bottles is heard, but Howie Newsome carries an imaginary milk bottle rack. He strokes Bessie, the imaginary horse drawing his imaginary wagon. Dr. Gibbs washes his hands in an imaginary sink.

The world of pretense continues, as Mr. Webb mows his lawn and George Webb plays baseball in the street. Ladders are used to represent the bedrooms of George and Emily which are on the second floors of the adjacent homes. The two teenagers mount these ladders to do their studying. When his father calls him, George dismounts the ladder and goes downstairs (stage level) to receive his father's subtle lecture in the kitchen, represented by the tables and chairs. When George's sister, Rebecca, retires, she goes up the same ladder.

As the second act opens, the tables and chairs of the two kitchens still occupy the stage. The same pretenses of the first act are once again employed: imaginary sinks, newspapers, etc. In the drugstore scene, the Stage Manager puts a board across the backs of two of the kitchen chairs and brings in two bar stools. The Stage Manager, acting in the role of a druggist-soda jerk, draws water and soda from imaginary faucets and scoops imaginary ice cream. In their turn, George and Emily sip the sodas through imaginary straws.

At a signal from the Stage Manager, stagehands replace the soda fountain and kitchen props with church pews. A small platform is used for the pulpit and a slide of a stained-glass window projected on the back wall complete the church imagery.

Between the second and third acts the Stage Manager arranges three rows of twelve chairs to simulate the cemetery on the hill. The empty chair in the front row will soon be occupied by Emily. The knees of the dead symbolize the gravestones. Actual props in the act include the handkerchief Sam Craig uses to wipe his forehead after digging the grave, the umbrellas used by Joe Stoddard and a little later by the people in the funeral procession.

The mourners follow four men carrying an imaginary coffin and gather around an imaginary grave. When Emily returns to the day of her twelfth birthday, the audience is given a capsule review of all the imaginary props and scenes of the earlier part of the play, the morning newspaper, the milk bottles, the breakfast scene, a blue hair ribbon, the birthday gift from her father, and the kitchen stove.

When we recall Wilder's dramatic belief in the necessity of pretense, we enjoy the play even more. In "Introduction to Three Plays," Wilder himself referred to Chinese drama where an actor rides a stick to simulate a horse and Japanese Noh drama where a player walks around the stage to simulate a long journey. He calls upon collaboration by the audience to achieve **realism** in *Our Town*. This technique is as old as drama itself. It is only the motion-picture **epic** or the elaborateness of contemporary dramatic production which makes an audience expect more. In the great plays of the Greeks the battle scenes and murders, or any other complicated scenes take place off stage. The same is true with the plays of William Shakespeare. The great battle scenes are reported to the audience by messengers or participants. When a Shakespearean scene does take place on the field of battle, it is usually within a tent or on the parapet of a fortress. The world of pretense is an integral, enjoyable, and successful part of *Our Town*, and according to Wilder's dramatic credo, it has been an integral, enjoyable, and successful part of great drama through the ages.

TOWARD OUR TOWN

Wilder used the technique of pretense in many of the three-minute, one act plays he wrote before *Our Town*. By the time he wrote this play, he had refined and polished the device of imaginary props. In *The Long Christmas Dinner* (1931), he has his characters sit through ninety Christmas dinners. They eat from imaginary plates with imaginary knives and forks. The passage of time is shown through Wilder's collaborators, the actors, who are allowed wigs to show their rapidly increasing age, but who must still rely mainly on their acting ability to achieve a realistic production. He also uses no curtain in this play, so that as the audience enters, its views a half-lit stage with a table set sumptuously for Christmas dinner.

PULLMAN CAR HIAWATHA

There are also many parallels of stagecraft between *Our Town* and *Pullman Car Hiawatha* (1931). *Pullman Car Hiawatha* does use a curtain and the limited scenery of a balcony or bridge, which runs the length of the back wall of the stage. Two flights of stairs lead down to the stage. The most obvious similarity between the plays is that they both use a Stage Manager to suggest images of the scenes. The same informality and directness that pervades his role in *Our Town,* is present in the Stage Manager of *Pullman Car Hiawatha* who tells the audience that the stage is a pullman car named "Hiawatha" (a friendly chief of the Mohawk Indians, made famous by Henry Wadsworth Longfellow's poem of the same name). He further informs his audience that this car is on the New York to Chicago run and draws the dimensions of the berths and compartments on the floor of the stage with a piece of chalk just as the Stage Manager in *Our Town* arranges the two kitchens. As the actors enter they carry their own chairs which are used to simulate the berths and compartments of the car.

Wilder personifies the places which the train passes in the night. Interestingly, one of the towns is named Grover's Corners, Ohio. A boy personifies this town of 821 people and coyly recites a Sunday School exercise. A man in shirt sleeves symbolizes a field; a tramp arises from the rails for humor; the wife and children of an alcoholic represent Parkersburg, Ohio, population 2,604; a mechanic, weather forecaster, a watchman in a tower, and the ghost of a dead trestle worker also parade out on the balcony, recite their pieces and leave. Now that the geographical location of the pullman car is known, the Stage Manager calls forth personifications of the hours so that we know the time as well as the location. In one of his most beautiful epigrammatic lines, Wilder creates the **metaphor** that "the minutes are gossips, the hours are philosophers, and the years theologians." The only exception is the hour of midnight which is also a theologian. The hours unwind across the balcony; Plato is ten o'clock, Epictetus is eleven o'clock, and St. Augustine is twelve o'clock. After the hours leave, the Stage Manager calls forth the planets, each of whom makes his own distinctive sound. Finally, two archangels dressed in blue serge suits come down and remove a woman passenger. She attempts to resist, but finally she assents, bidding farewell by employing many of the same details which Emily uses in her farewell scene at the end of *Our Town*. They both say good-by to their hometowns, to their mothers and fathers, and finally to subjective symbols which have a deep and personal meaning only to themselves. One need only compare the two passages, published nearly eight years apart, to see that Emily's farewell to life is far superior in artistic merit and dramatic craftsmanship to that of her counterpart on the train. However, the death of both characters is the **climax** of the respective plays. There is a clear indication in *Pullman Car*

Hiawatha that the dead woman is going to heaven, but in *Our Town,* we never go physically, philosophically, or theologically beyond a personified graveyard.

Another parallel between the two plays is the way in which the Stage Manager fits the play into the continuum of time. In *Pullman Car Hiawatha* we proceed from the places the train passes, to the time, to the solar system, to heaven itself, the theological symbol of eternity. In *Our Town,* only one character, and a minor one at that, is used to list the same connection between microscopic Grover's Corners and all history, philosophy, and eternity. Rebecca Gibbs tells her brother about a letter received by a schoolmate from her minister. It was addressed to the girl's name, the farm where she lived, the town, the county, the state, the country, the continent, the hemisphere, the Earth, the solar system, the universe, and finally the mind of God. Wilder did not use the philosophers or theologians to pinpoint the time of day in *Our Town* as he did in *Pullman Car Hiawatha.* He has the Stage Manager tell us the time of day directly; the Stage Manager also gives us geographical details and meteorological information when it is necessary in the story.

Before we continue our discussion of *Our Town,* a few final words on *Pullman Car Hiawatha* may be helpful. When the archangels come to lead the woman up the stairs on to the balcony and finally offstage, there are no earthly sounds except for the sleeping passengers in the pullman car. When the dead woman and angels leave, the Stage Manager once again calls out the personified towns, the mechanic symbol of weather, the philosophic hours, and the onomatopoetic planets. He conducts all these sounds in a symphony of the earth's and, of course, life's sounds. Reality is restored as the train arrives in Chicago. But softly in the background while the passengers go about their business, the minutes and hours tick on, and the planets continue their interminable revolutions. We sense this cycle beginning again as the cleaning women prepare the train for its return to New York. In the same way the quantities mentioned in *Our Town,* the thousands of times the sun has risen, the forty thousand meals one of the characters has prepared, the fifty thousand meals of an average marriage, and the **allusion** by the undertaker to the fact that new parts of the cemetery are being opened all the time, all contribute to emphasize Wilder's historical and archetypal view that these little things, and yes, even the major ones, such as marriage and death, will happen over and over and over again in the course of time.

MUSIC IN OUR TOWN

Early in the play, editor Webb, while describing culture in Grover's Corners, laments that while there are a few girls at the high school who play the piano, they don't seem to enjoy it very much. Also, he says, most people in Grover's Corners are familiar with Handel's "Largo." Besides these musical allusions, there are several places in the play where music is an actual part of the scenes. "Blessed Be The Tie That Binds" is the only selection which appears in all three acts. In Act I, it is sung at choir practice, and later Mr. Webb whistles the tune. In Act II, it is part of the music at George and Emily's wedding, and in Act III it is sung by the mourners at Emily's graveside. It can definitely be considered one of the unifying elements of the play. This traditional Christian hymn reflects the trials and tribulations of life and how they will be assuaged by the perfect love of God in eternity.

At the choir practice there is a **foreshadowing** of the music which will be heard at the wedding scene in Act II. Simon Stimson, the church organist, announces that the choir will sing the same music at Fred Hersey's wedding this week that was used at Jane Trowbridge's last month. Weddings are the most staid and traditional of the archetypal ceremonies in life. At Emily's wedding, Simon plays the familiar entrance hymn from Lohengrin and the familiar exit hymn, Mendelssohn's "Wedding March." At the wedding, the choir also sings, "Love Divine, All Love Excelling" and once again, "Blessed Be The Tie That Binds." Another traditional hymn, "Art Thou Weary, Art Thou Languid" is practiced by the choir in Act I. Wilder's use of these familiar pieces of church music fits in perfectly with his description of Grover's Corners as a symbolic small American town. Their popularity also helps the play achieve universal audience appeal.

SOUND EFFECTS IN OUR TOWN

Like the scenery, sound effects in *Our Town* are kept to a minimum. Only those sounds familiar to a typical small American town in the early 1900s are heard. Since the story begins at dawn, the crowing of a rooster is heard. Soon the whistle from the 5:45 train heading toward Boston is heard. The sounds of Howie Newsome's horse and milk wagon and the clanking of imaginary milk bottles set the initial scene for morning greetings between the newspaper boy, the milkman, and Doc Gibbs. Later in the morning we hear the factory whistle from the Cartwright factory, the sounds of the children going to school, and the sounds of Mrs. Gibbs feeding the chickens. During the afternoon we hear Mr. Webb mowing his lawn and the children being let out of school at 3:00. The evening is highlighted by the musical strains of the church choir and the sounds of the crickets end the rural and moonlit setting of Act I. Many sounds are left to the pretenses of images created by the Stage Manager. Some of the visual and sound images the Stage Manager creates, but which are never really seen or heard, include the town's first automobile, owned by Mr. Cartwright, the banker, the construction sounds associated with the building of the new bank, the constable making his nightly rounds, the sounds of rain and thunder and other weather sounds which would call for intricate sound effects or elaborate and technical scenery.

WEATHER, SEASONS, AND NATURE IN OUR TOWN

As it does in everyone's life, weather plays an important part in the play. In Act I, "Daily Life", the opening conversation is concerned with weather. The weather of Act I is a fine spring day. Doc Gibbs has just delivered twins to Mrs. Goruslawski. The two trellises which represent the Gibbs' and Webb's homes are covered with flowers. The Stage Manager describes Mrs. Gibbs' vegetable garden and Mrs. Webb's sunflowers. He comments that the imaginary flower gardens are enough scenery for those in the audience who think they need some scenery. Later in the morning Mrs. Gibbs and Mrs. Webb sit outside their homes stringing beans which Mrs. Webb will can for the forthcoming winter. Several of the characters comment on the beautiful moonlight that evening. The smell of heliotrope permeates the air and the sound of crickets chirping completes the final scene of a beautiful day and evening - May 7, 1901.

In Act II, which the Stage Manager calls "Love and Marriage," we think of Mark Twain's anecdote about New England weather, "If you don't like it, just wait a minute." The act opens early on the morning of July 7, 1904, the day of George and Emily's wedding. It has been raining and thundering most of the night. The gardens are soaked but the rain has stopped for a little while. The Stage Manager notes that over a thousand days of winter and summer, spring and fall have come and gone since that last act. We learn that Constable Warren is worried that the river may overflow because of so much rain. Most of the early conversation in this act also concerns the weather. Because of the wedding, Mrs. Gibbs and Mrs. Webb are quite anxious, but it looks as if it will clear for the ceremony. Mrs. Gibbs makes George put on his rubbers before he leaves the house, and on the way across the yard to Emily's house he skips imaginary puddles. The flashback to George and Emily's courtship scene is also set on a fine spring day. At the conclusion of the act, a bright light is put on the bride and groom, now man and wife, as they leave the church. The pretense easily allows us to picture the rain soaked and damp day giving way to rays and heat of the afternoon sun.

The Stage Manager never directly tells us the title of Act III, but we can safely assume it is "Death." It is nine years later, the scene is the cemetery, and Emily had died while giving birth to her second child. At the beginning of the act, the Stage Manager gives one of his most beautiful descriptions in a passage describing the cemetery. It is on a windy hilltop, set off during the day by the sun, the sky, and clouds, and in the evening, by the moon and the stars. When you stand there, you can see the surrounding mountains and valleys, the streams and towns for many miles. Mountain laurel and lilacs give the location its color. The Stage Manager describes it so that it appears as a natural part of the landscape, something which belongs more to nature than to the artificial and man-made towns which speckle the valleys around it. Once again, it is raining as Emily's funeral procession makes its way slowly up the hill. The mourners stand together, huddled under their umbrellas. Mrs. Soames, one of the dead, comments on the muddy road when she sees Emily. The conversation among the dead is still of the weather as Emily notices for the first time that it is raining and the dead state in unison that it is getting colder. In a touching scene among the living at the funeral, Doctor Gibbs takes one of the flowers from

Emily's grave and places it on the grave of his wife, Julia, who had died a few years before. In the flashback scene when Emily relives her twelfth birthday - February 11, 1899 - we have our only New England winter scene. It is not one of skiing, skating, or winter carnival, but rather one which points out the hardships of that season. It has snowed for almost a week, a man had nearly frozen to death, the temperature is ten below zero, and George has trudged across the backyards to leave Emily's birthday present on the back porch. When the scene changes back to the present and Emily says good-by to the world, one of the things she specifically mentions are her mother's sunflowers. As the play ends the Stage Manager tells us that the weather is clearing and the stars are coming out to continue their eternal orbits.

ALLUSIONS IN OUR TOWN

An author uses the literary device of **allusions** when he wishes to refer the reader to a person or thing which will add a new dimension to what he is saying. For example, in Leon Uris' book, *Exodus*, we immediately recognize the Biblical **allusion** to the title of the second book of the Old Testament where Moses leads the people of Israel out of bondage in Egypt and to the promised land. With this knowledge the reader enjoys *Exodus* all the more as he draws his own parallels between the ancient odyssey to the promised land and the more modern one described by Leon Uris.

The **allusions** in *Our Town* are, for the most part, familiar and easy to understand. When Professor Willard describes Grover's Corners he alludes to its geological make-up - the town rests on Pleistocene granite in the Appalachian range. It has some Devonian basalt and Mesozoic shale. These **allusions** help to show that the land has been here for millions of years.

With **allusions** to Amerindian inhabitants and brachiocephalic English settlers, the professor is merely referring to the original Indians of the area and later the English colonists who settled the area. Wilder has the professor use these terms so that he can give archaeological, geological, and historical dimension to Grover's Corners and at the same time characterize Professor Willard as a pedant.

The **allusions** used by editor Webb in his social, political, religious, ethical, and cultural description of Grover's Corners are so comprehensive and general that it seems indeed that it could be our town which he is describing. The Stage Manager's discussion of what the townspeople are going to put in the time capsule, which will be placed in the cornerstone of the new Cartwright bank and opened a thousand or more years from now, reads like a short course in the history of man. He alludes to the great civilizations of Babylonia, Greece, and Rome, and comments on how little we have left of these high-water marks of history - especially of the common people. What the people of Grover's Corners will put in the time capsule is a fine indication of their character. They want to include copies of *The New York Times,* Mr. Webb's *Sentinel,* the Bible, "The Constitution of the United States," and the plays of William Shakespeare. With this list we can perhaps imagine Grovers' Corners' cultural connection with the rest of the world and with history itself; but more important, we get an idea from these **allusions** of what is important to the people of this symbolic and representative little town.

There are some **allusions** in the play which are less obvious than the ones we have mentioned above. Some of these include references by the questioners in the audience to the problems of alcoholism, culture, social protest; others to the field of psychology and how the simplest way to avoid a nervous breakdown is to work hard; to the romantic philosophy of Rousseau; and finally one in which the Stage Manager alludes to a poem by Edgar Lee Masters which deals with the paradoxes of life. The casualness and informality of style in *Our Town* cause the **allusions** to blend in perfectly with the dialogue of the Stage Manager and the other characters. Understanding them adds a rich and worthwhile perspective to this play, or for that matter to any literary work which employs this technique.

COLLOQUIALISM AND HUMOR IN OUR TOWN

The casualness and informality of the Stage Manager, who wears a hat and lights his pipe before speaking to the audience, prepares us for the warm colloquialism of the play. The only elevated or stuffy language is used by Professor Willard, and, interestingly enough, he is one of the few satirized characters in the play. The technique Wilder uses is understatement. Vast areas of history, complicated philosophical movements, and delicate theological propositions are discussed in colloquial fashion, and then either dropped completely or resolved to the present satisfaction of the character and audience. For example, the Stage Manager alludes to the political philosophies of Jean Jacques Rousseau by talking about what some French fellow said. There is no great lack of reality, no significant theological thesis approved or denied when we hear the dead talk among themselves and Emily relives her twelfth birthday. Wilder has acknowledged his indebtedness to Dante for this particular idea. The apparent omniscience of the Stage Manager as he looks both forward to 1930 when Dr. Gibbs dies and backward in time to the town's founding fathers and even before, becomes quite plausible after the first few minutes of the play have passed.

The colloquial speech gives both the Stage Manager and the other citizens of "Grover's Corners their best dimension of reality. Phrases like "the hull town," "fella," stummick ain't what it used to be," and "it brung 'em a fortune" are among the hundreds of words and phrases which create the New England dialect. Certain typically New England expressions are also employed. For example, Wilder has characters refer to lunch time as "dinner" and describe the weather as "potato weather."

Our Town is rich in homey humor. The provincialism of Grover's Corners and people in general is shown by their characteristic interest in things which effect only their isolated lives and not the whole world or even the town as a whole. There are many examples: that Joe Crowell's most important news of the day is that his teacher is leaving town to marry a man in Concord, or that Buffalo is "out west," or Simon Stimson's statement that his choir couldn't outsing the Methodists if they tried. The humor is successful, because, like the dialogue, it is informal, wholesome, and colloquial. It does not detract from the dignity of man, yet it shows his imperfections in a tasteful manner. In the only scene where the humor is in poor taste (the baseball players kidding George at his wedding), the Stage Manager quickly steps in and controls it forcefully but tactfully.

THEME AND UNIVERSALITY

The **theme** of a work of art is the meaning or idea which the artist is trying to convey. The **theme** of *Our Town* is that living persons never really appreciate all the wonderful things of life, especially the thousands of minute experiences which go to make up our everyday living. A secondary theme, strongly implied in the play, is that this problem is true of all men in all times - therefore, the meaning is universal. As a humanist, a lover of mankind, Wilder celebrates the common man and the common activities of that man. He transforms the ordinary scenes of rising, eating breakfast, going to work or school, coming home, eating again, relaxing or doing homework, and finally going to bed again, to the level of ritual a sequential celebration of the rites of life. Unlike many of his contemporaries who satirized, revolted against, or lamented symbolic Grover's Corners (from Sinclair Lewis' "Gopher Prairie" to Sherwood Anderson's "Winesburg, Ohio," and from Edgar Lee Masters "Spoon River" to Edwin Arlington Robinson's "Tilbury Town," and from William Faulkner's "Jefferson" the seat of "Yoknapatawpha County" to Edith Wharton's "Starkfield" in *Ethan Frome*), Wilder points to these little, everyday experiences as the very things we would miss if we reflected on life after we had died in the manner in which Emily does at the end of the play. Emily regrets, she never lived life more fully, appreciating every tiny and precious detail of everything she ever experienced. Her reflections remind us of the beginning of William Wordsworth's famous sonnet:

The world is too much with us, Getting and spending, we lay waste our powers: Little we see in Nature that is ours; We have given our hearts away, a sordid boon!

Whereas Wordsworth is concerned with man's seeing too little in Nature and being the victim of a material and economic world, Emily and the other dead in *Our Town* are concerned with man's seeing too little in life itself. Simon Stimson, for instance, sees life as a valley of darkness and ignorance through which man travels on his short journey, constantly "laying waste his powers" and constantly being subjected to the weakening habits of his passions, specifically, in Simon's case, alcohol.

In addition to celebrating these seemingly mundane aspects of life, Wilder uses another interesting technique to support his **theme**. He makes the normal salutations of everyday conversations - the "hellos," "good-bys," "how are yous," and "how's the weather" a litany of the wonders of life. Yet how little we really think about these things which we ask and answer countless times every day of our lives. Some people say that the tragedy in *Our Town* is that the characters are not interested in anything beyond the limits of Grover's Corners. Even if this is an accurate observation, sometimes discounted by the few who occasionally leave the town (for example, Joe Crowell, Jr., who is killed in the First World War, Miss Foster who marries and moves to Concord, and Rebecca Gibbs who also marries and moves to Canton, Ohio), the fact remains that the people of Grover's Corners are human beings and will not experience life any less intensely than any other man in any other place at any other time.

The three areas of life - "daily life," "love and marriage," and "death" which Wilder chooses to bring into focus in this play are three areas which are of paramount importance and interest to any sensitive human being. It is in this archetypal dimension that the play achieves its universality. A wideness of appeal is created which reaches not only to American audiences, past and present, but to foreign audiences and readers as well.

In "A Preface to Three Plays" (1957), Wilder points to the symbolic nature of Grover's Corners, as set against the wider symbols of time and space. The author emphasizes the largeness of the numbers used throughout the play. For example, the Stage Manager doesn't say that three years have passed but rather that the sun has risen over a thousand times. When the Stage Manager describes the industriousness of Mrs. Gibbs and Mrs. Webb, he talks in terms of the thousands of meals they have cooked in their lives as housewives. In describing the town at one point he says that all 2,642 of the town's inhabitants have eaten dinner and all those dishes have been washed. Commenting on the forthcoming marriage of George and Emily, he humorously describes that state as the sharing of 50,000 meals with someone. Wilder's purpose here is to give the play the necessary dimensions to make its meaning applicable not only to one man but to every man.

INTRODUCTION TO THE CHARACTERS OF OUR TOWN

Stage Manager: The narrator of the Play who also acts as moderator when the audience questions the characters. He freely enters and leaves the dialogue. Also he doubles as a druggist, soda jerk, a clergyman, and a woman in the street.

Dr. Frank Gibbs: The town doctor.

Joe Crowell: A newspaperboy.

Howie Newsome: A milkman.

Julia Gibbs: The doctor's wife.

Myrtle Webb: The editor's wife.

George Gibbs: The doctor's son.

Rebecca Gibbs: His sister.

Wally Webb: The editor's son.

Emily Webb: The editor's daughter.

Professor Willard: A historian from the state university.

Mr. Charles Webb: Editor of the town newspaper.

Woman in the Balcony: The representative of temperance.

Man in the Auditorium: The representative of social protest.

Lady in the Box: The representative of culture.

Simon Stimson: The church organist.

Louella Soames: The town gossip.

Constable Warren: The town policeman.

Si Crowell: Joe's brother, also a newspaperboy.

Three Baseball Players: George's high school teammates.

Sam Craig: A cousin of the Webbs.

Joe Stoddard: The town undertaker.

Mr. Carter: One of the dead.

OTHER CHARACTERS MENTIONED BY THE PLAYERS

Julia Hersey: Mrs. Gibbs maiden name.

Shorty Hawkins: The station master.

Mr. Cartwright: The town banker and richest citizen.

Miss Foster: A school teacher who marries and moves to Concord.

Mrs. Goruslawski: Dr. Gibbs' patient who gives birth to twins.

Bessie: Howie Newsome's horse.

Hester Wilcox: A cousin of Mrs. Gibbs.

Silas Peckham, Uncle Luke, Farmer McCartny: Local farmers,

Ellery Greenough: The stable owner.

Miss Corcoran: Emily's social studies teacher.

Fred Hersey, Jane Trowbridge: Weddings at which the choir sang.

Dr. Ferguson: A minister.

Mrs. Fairchild: A "citified" woman who locks her door.

Jane Crofut: A school chum of Rebecca's.

Hank Todd: The town's baseball hero twenty years ago.

Ernestine, Helen, Fred, Bob, Herb, Lizzy: High school friends of George and Emily.

Tom Hawkins: Driver of the hardware store wagon.

Carey Craig: Julia Gibbs' sister.

Mr. Wilkins: Principal of the high school.

Mrs. Carter: A neighbor who cares for Emily's four-year old son the day of her funeral.

Aunt Norah: Emily's aunt.

The Lockharts: A family which moves away.

Professor Gruber: A meteorologist.

Irma, Martha, Mr. Foster, Mrs. Slocum: Members of the choir.

Mrs. Ellis: A customer at the drugstore.

Mrs. Wentworth: A patient of Dr. Gibbs.

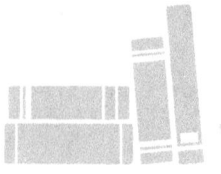

OUR TOWN

PLOT ANALYSIS

ACT I

Setting: Main street in Grover's Corners, New Hampshire. Kitchen and yards of the Gibbs' and Webb's homes.

Time: Morning, afternoon, and evening of May 7, 1901, a typical day in Grover's Corners.

The Stage Manager gives an introduction to the play by telling who wrote it, who produced it, who directed it, and who the actors are. The story takes place in Grover's Corners, New Hampshire, and the Stage Manager even gives the exact latitude and longitude of the town. Walking freely around the stage like a sightseeing guide, he describes the physical layout of the town. He begins with the breaking dawn and the mountains which surround the town and describes imaginary churches and ethnic groups, and the principal municipal building which houses the town hall, post office, and jail. At this point the Stage Manager jumps ahead in time and tells us that the first automobile will come down Main Street in 1906. He also tells us that Doc Gibbs dies in 1930 and the new hospital is named after him. He points out the homes of the two main families in the play, the Webbs and the Gibbs. The homes are very much alike, with trees and flowers, trellises to simulate their back doors, and tables and chairs to represent their kitchens. Returning to the side of the stage, the Stage Manager narrator sums up our town (Grover's Corners) as a "nice town." He alludes to the cemetery on the hill, some of whose gravestones go back to the late 1600s; some of the descendants of these early settlers are still prominent in the town.

As the dialogue begins, Doc Gibbs is returning from delivering twins to Mrs. Goruslawski in Polish town. Doc Gibbs exchanges greetings and weather news with Joe Crowell, Jr., the paperboy, and Howie Newsome, the milkman. Mrs. Gibbs is preparing breakfast, calling her children, George, age 16, and Rebecca, age 11, for school. The action switches to the kitchen next door where Mrs. Webb is also calling her children for school. The Webb children are Emily, age 16, and Wally, age 11. Mrs. Gibbs complains to her husband that George's only interest these days is baseball and he is not doing his chores. As a factory whistle is heard the children rush out through their respective trellises as they leave for school. Both women stress the motherly concern over table manners, neatness in dress, and good health to their children between the time they come down to breakfast and leave for school. Later in the morning Mrs. Gibbs and Mrs. Webb chat about health, winter canning, antiques, vacations, choir practice, and their husbands. They have a wonderful neighborly relationship.

The Stage Manager interrupts to continue his description of Grover's Corners. He is aided by Professor Willard who lectures on the archaeological, geological, sociological, and historical background of the town. The population is 2,642 people. Mr. Webb, editor of *The Grover's Corners Sentinel*, a morning newspaper published twice a week, discusses the ethical, political, and social aspects of the town. In response to questions from the audience, he also talks about drinking, social protest, and culture in Grover's Corners.

Once again the Stage Manager breaks in to comment on a typical afternoon in this quiet town. George takes a few minutes away from baseball to walk Emily home from school. Since their bedrooms are across from each other, he suggests that they set up some sort of telegraph system so that Emily can help him with algebra. Emily consents to help him but only with hints, not answers. At home Emily chats with her mother about school and beauty. Emily is anxious that she is not good looking. The Stage Manager reports on the contents which will go into the time capsule in the cornerstone of the new Cartwright bank. They include *The New York Times, The Grover's Corners Sentinel,* the Bible, the Constitution, the works of William Shakespeare, and a copy of this play so that some future residents - one or two thousand years from now - will have some idea of how the people in Grover's Corners lived and loved and died at the beginning of the twentieth century.

As the final part of Act I begins, George and Emily climb two ladders which simulate the second floor bedrooms in their respective homes. Choir practice is conducted by Simon Stimson, the church organist. Emily helps George with his homework and they both show all the signs of "puppy love." Doc Gibbs calls George downstairs to lecture him about helping his mother by doing his chores. On the way home from choir practice, Mrs. Gibbs, Mrs. Webb, and Mrs. Soames, the town gossip, talk about Simon Stimson who has a drinking problem. Once home, Mrs. Gibbs and her husband talk over the day's happenings. Upstairs, George is "struck" by the wonderful moonlight. Downtown Constable Warren and editor Webb talk about the town and

Simon Stimson. When Mr. Webb gets home he finds Emily meditating on the wonderful moonlight. In the final event in the first act Rebecca tells George about a uniquely addressed letter her friend Jane Crofut received from her minister.

Comment

Many things are accomplished in the first act. We are introduced to the unusual role of the Stage-Manager-narrator who (1) describes the town with enough detail and universality to really make it seem like our town (2) introduces us, with a minimal amount of description, to the principal characters, and (3) hints at what will happen in the following scenes. The Stage Manager's informality and colloquial mannerism easily win the affection of the audience and make the whole play quite realistic.

"Daily Life" is the motivation of the entire act which is built around several scenes which happen every day. Wilder does not divide the play into scenes, but if for the sake of our discussion we were to do this, the following units would be apparent: the Main Street scene (where Doc Gibbs chats with the newsboy and the milkman), the breakfast scene in the Gibbs' home and the breakfast scene in the Webb's home, another Main Street scene (as the children leave for school), a backyard scene (where Mrs. Gibbs and Mrs. Webb have a neighborly chat), the lecture scene (where Professor Willard gives us background material on the town), a less formal lecture scene in the "fireside chat" tradition (where editor Webb gives us additional facts about the town), another Main Street scene (as the children return from school), a kitchen scene in the Webb house (as Mrs. Webb and Emily chat), a choir scene, the bedroom scene (as George gets hints on his homework from Emily), a kitchen scene (where Doc Gibbs talks to his son), another Main Street scene (as the women return from choir practice), the final scenes in the Gibb's house (as the doctor and his wife chat and George and Rebecca talk) and on Main Street (where Mr. Webb, Constable Warren, and Simon Stimson make their way home).

This emphasis on so many scenes taking place on Main street is not accidental. The center of every small town is one central street, and in the course of our comings and goings on an average day we will cross or shop or somehow have some contact with this center of our limited universe.

It is interesting to note how the author connects these seemingly insignificant activities in the daily lives of nondescript people in a small town at a particular time with the lives and activities of all men at all times past, present, and future. There are two places where this connection is clear. The first is the address on Jane Crofut's letter. It shows a direct succession of steps from God to the universe to the solar system to the Earth to the Western Hemisphere to the North American Continent to the United States to the state of New Hampshire to Sutton County to Grover's Corners to her very house and, of course, to Jane herself. This cosmic connection between an individual in his temporal and ephemeral state and God in his eternal state is part of the philosophy of the play. Man is part of something larger and greater than himself even if he is not always aware of it. Another place where Wilder fits Grover's Corners into the scheme of history is when the Stage Manager talks about the contents of the time capsule. One of the purposes of the play, he tells us, is to show other human beings how these human beings lived at this place and in this time. After all, each stage in history has transferred something to each successive stage, and it is not beyond belief that Grover's Corners also has its place in that great chain. While we recall the pyramids of Egypt, the temples of Greece, the conquests and armies and laws of the Romans, we forget many times that the millions and millions of people who have lived on the earth before us each had a "daily life" with its minute experiences, insignificant to us, but all important to them.

There is also a good deal of **foreshadowing** in this initial act. We are interested in what will happen to George and Emily, to Simon Stimson and his drinking problem, and to the doctor, editor, and their wives. The seemingly repetitive daily events of this act reflect similar scenes in all of our lives, wherever and whatever our towns might be.

ACT II

Setting: The Gibbs and Webb Homes; Main Street; Mr. Morgan's drugstore; the Congregational Church for the wedding ceremony.

Time: The morning and afternoon of July 7, 1904, the day of the wedding, and a flashback to a spring afternoon a year before.

The Stage Manager discusses the three years which have passed. Si Crowell, who has inherited his brother's paper route, Howie Newsome and Constable Warren open the dialogue by discussing the wedding. Once again we see a parallel development of the action, which alternates between the Gibbs' kitchen and the Webb's kitchen. Both Mrs. Gibbs and Mrs. Webb need extra milk from Howie Newsome so that they'll have enough for all the guests. Dr. Gibbs and Mrs. Gibbs are both anxious about George's marriage. But they soon realize that they weren't much older than George and Emily when they were married. They conclude that marriage is a natural thing; George and Emily will have their troubles but so does everyone else. Upstairs, Rebecca is crying. George is the only relaxed person in the Gibbs house hold as he leaves to go see Emily at seven o'clock. Mrs. Gibbs still makes him dress warmly so he won't catch cold. At Emily's house, Mrs. Webb naturally refuses to let the groom see the bride before the ceremony. George and Mr. Webb chat about superstition, customs, and the traditional views of married life and women. Mr. Webb relates some advice his father had given him on marriage and then tells George to ignore it. The whole conversation is characterized by pre-wedding nervousness.

The Stage Manager interrupts to give his views on marriage, and to take us back a year in time to a scene at Mr. Morgan's drugstore when George and Emily decide to get married. As they are coming home from school Emily tells George that he is conceited and she's not sure she likes him anymore. Emily is on the verge of tears, so George invites her to have an ice cream soda at Mr. Morgan's drugstore. The Stage Manager plays Mr. Morgan. This has also been the day on which George was elected president of the junior class and Emily has been elected secretary and treasurer. George tells Mr. Morgan a fib to cover up the real reason for Emily's tears. As George and Emily discuss their future, George decides to abandon his plans for attending Agricultural College and go directly to work on his Uncle Luke's farm. In a nervous and awkwardly sensitive statement of affection and love, George tells Emily that he loves her and wants to marry her. But at no time does he use the direct words or phrases usually associated with such an important decision.

The final portion of Act II takes place in the Church. The Stage Manager plays the part of the minister and comments on all the weddings at which he has officiated. All the major characters have a part in the wedding. Mrs. Webb cries that her daughter is too young to get married. George's teammates make fun of him until they are stopped by the Stage Manager. George panics at the last minute but is helped by his mother; Emily also panics but is aided by her father. The traditional wedding music is played by Simon Stimson and sung by the choir. Mrs. Soames gossips, interrupting the service. But all these pre-wedding jitters and interruptions are abated as the Stage Manager-minister performs the ceremony and George and Emily leave the Church in a burst of sunlight.

Comment

This act contains a charming and humorous description of one of mankind's most traditional social institutions - marriage. We follow the development of George and Emily's love through various stages from the "puppy love" sequence of Act I to the tender and emotionally charged teenage courtship scene at Mr. Morgan's drugstore. The young and idealistic lovers proceed confidently into marriage only to panic at the last moment. But with reassurance from their parents, they survive the hectic experience of the wedding day itself and successfully begin their lives together. Many modern students find it hard to believe that George would give up college to marry Emily. It must be remembered that the pressures for a college education were not as great in the early twentieth century as they are today. While their parents do show anxiety over such an early marriage, they give in when they realize they themselves weren't much older when they were married and everyone has a right to his own problems. The ups and downs of their courtship, the reactions of the parents, and the church wedding are all familiar and realistic scenes. They make up the most humorous parts of the play, especially when Mr. Webb tries to explain the feminine aspect of marital bliss to his future son-in-law.

The Stage Manager not only plays his usual role in this act, but also assumes the roles of the philosophical Mr. Morgan, the town druggist, and the minister who marries the young couple. These three roles give the narrator an excellent opportunity to express many ideas on "love and marriage." His basic premise is that almost everyone gets married, and in Grover's Corners the usual time is immediately after high school commencement. Colloquially he calls the custom part of a vicious circle. Early in the act he alludes to "Lucinda Matlock," a poem which appears in *Spoon River Anthology* by Edgar Lee Masters. The poem tells a story parallel in many ways to some of the women in *Our Town*. Lucinda lived to the age of ninety-six. She met Davis Matlock at a dance, fell in love and soon married him. They lived a full life together, spanning seventy years during which they had twelve children, eight of whom were dead by the time Lucinda was sixty. Lucinda is shocked to hear younger people complaining about life. She worked hard all her life, knew sorrow and happiness, sickness and health, and loved life all the more for her ninety-six years.

At some point in this act, each character gives his opinion on George and Emily's marriage. Si Crowell is disturbed because George is giving up baseball to marry Emily; Mrs. Gibbs and Mrs. Webb find it very difficult to let go of their children: Dr. Gibbs and Mr. Webb find it difficult also, but as might be expected, control themselves better than their wives. The Stage Manager symbolizes the years of a marriage in terms of the number of meals the couple will share. For example, a couple married for fifty years would share nearly 50,000 meals. By using this symbol, the author is able to underscore one of the little things of life which make life so precious. Yet how often do we think of the number of meals, or smokes or naps we enjoy in a lifetime? It reminds one of T. S. Eliot's "Prufrock" who measured his life in coffee spoons.

George and Emily's youth, idealism, and optimism are emphasized in the courtship scene at the drugstore. George has just been elected class president and Emily has been elected secretary and treasurer. George will soon face a turning point in his life. The actual decision to marry is achieved by inference and understatement. George and Emily have always been together and neither would like it any other way. The philosophy of Mr. Morgan, the druggist, is concerned with the major changes on Main Street as automobiles slowly replace the horse and buggies. Perhaps this is fitting as George and Emily prepare to take their places in the new adult generation of Grover's Corners. As the Stage Manager hinted at the beginning of this act, it starts the vicious circle all over again. "Vicious circle" in this sense means chain of events.

At the Church scene, the Stage Manager stresses the sacredness and confusions of the wedding ceremony. He has assumed the role of the minister because he is interested in the quality of people. He again states his major point - that people were meant to live by twos. Near the end of the ceremony, the Stage Manager reviews the whole life cycle following marriage - Sunday afternoons, children, picnics and rides, grandchildren, illness, and old age. This last reference also foreshadows the action in Act III.

ACT III

Setting: The Grover's Corners Cemetery.

Time: The summer of 1913, the day of Emily's funeral and a flashback to February 11, 1899, the date of Emily's twelfth birthday.

The Stage Manager describes the Grover's Corners Cemetery where most of the action in this act takes place. It is the day of Emily's funeral; she had died at the age of 26 while giving birth to her second child. The Stage Manager and, later, the characters, comment on the gravestones which symbolize an autobiography of the community. As the dialogue begins Sam Craig, who has returned from Buffalo, New York for the funeral, talks with Joe Stoddard, the undertaker. Their conversation reveals the fates of many of the characters. Julia Gibbs died three years before and Simon Stimson committed suicide. The Stage Manager tells us of the death of young Wally Webb while on a scouting trip. The dead who sit on neatly arranged rows of chairs also carry on a commentary about the living. As Emily's mourners, including George, Doc Gibbs, and the Webbs, stand at her graveside, she too joins the dead and assumes a previously empty chair in the front row. She is greeted by Mrs. Gibbs, Mrs. Soames, and Simon Stimson. The general attitude of the dead is expressed in a set of paradoxes - life was good and bad, wonderful and awful, meaningful and sweet, yet bitter and terrible. Emily and her mother-in-law chat matter-of-factly about the farm and George and events in Grover's Corners. She doesn't feel like she is dead, and much to the distress of her fellow dead, she requests of the Stage Manager that she return to the day of her twelfth birthday.

The flashback scene of the morning of February 11, 1899, is reminiscent of the first act of the play. Her mother calls her for breakfast; the milkman, paperboy and constable chat about the weather; she receives birthday presents from her mother and father, her brother and George. But Emily sees that each minute of this typical day among the living is so precious and wonderful that she can't bear it, and so she returns to her new home among the dead. She recites a litany of good-bys to the things in life she will miss - the world of Grover's Corners, her mother and father, flowers, clocks, coffee, dresses, baths, and sleep, etc. - all the things which we tend to take for granted in life. Emily asks the Stage Manager if anyone really appreciates life while they are living it. His reply is that only the saints and poets do, and then only sometimes. George returns to the cemetery and shows his grief as he kneels next to Emily's grave. Emily pities him because he cannot really appreciate all the precious little things of life while he lives. As he did in the first act, the Stage Manager ends the play as most of the people in Grover's Corners go to sleep and the stars replace the rainy and cloudy skies of the past few days.

Comment

While there has been a **foreshadowing** of death throughout the first two acts, the death of Emily still comes as a shock. The reaction of the undertaker whose business is death is the best comment on the tragic event: Death is always present, but it is always sadder when the person is young. Wilder's use of chairs as graves and the knees of the dead as gravestones is the best pretension in the play. The Stage Manager softens the sadness somewhat when he only hints at the title for this act.

His commentary on the changes in the social customs of Grover's Corners in the thirteen years which the play has spanned are brief - more people are driving Fords and the twilight of the horse and buggy is at hand; more people are locking their doors at night. We can use the term which Doc Gibbs used at the beginning of the play and say that Grover's Corners is becoming more "citified." In his tour of the cemetery the narrator cites gravestones of the Revolutionary War and Civil War dead - men who died far away to protect a way of life. Wilder's archaeological background is seen when the Stage

Manager says that the history of man is in layers. On the subject of death, the Stage Manager discusses the first grief and many times the long sorrow, but concludes that life has a way of making us forget the dead as we are caught up once again in the hectic pace. The interesting twist that Wilder uses in this act is that not only do we, the living, soon forget the dead, but they also soon forget us. They seem to become united with the quietude of the cemetery and its setting, and soon the trials and tribulation of life seem distant and they achieve their well earned peace.

Wilder has borrowed this technique of using the afterlife from Dante's Purgatorio. In the theology of Christianity, purgatory is the place where the soul is "purged" of any remaining sin before it enters heaven. While there is no actual purgation among the characters in the Grover's Corners cemetery, there is a rapid and marked disinterest with the problems and anxieties of life. Mrs. Gibbs, for instance, is quite apathetic about life; she does not even comment when she sees her husband take a flower from Emily's grave and place it on hers. It is the expression on Doc Gibbs face which makes Emily realize how troubled life is.

The **theme** of the play - that we can never fully appreciate the precious gift of life - is developed when Emily returns to her place among the dead after reliving her twelfth birthday. As she bids farewell to many of the symbols of life which held meaning for her, she learns that perhaps the only people who have the vision to see life as she is now seeing it are the saints and poets. Sometimes even they fail to fully comprehend its meaning. Wilder's judgment of the dead, as seen by Mrs. Soames and Simon Stimson, is that they forget about living, just as the living eventually forget them. At the end of the play, the stars come out and Grover's Corners goes to sleep. These symbols show that the universe continues and Grover's Corners will begin another day at dawn. If there is a message in the play, it is one of faith in mankind, his failure to appreciate the precious little things of his life, and that tomorrow some of us will arise in our town and continue our parts in the "vicious circle."

OUR TOWN

CHARACTER ANALYSES

STAGE MANAGER

The Stage Manager is a man of many roles, but his tone and attitude in whatever role he is playing is about the same. He is informal, colloquial, and a homey philosopher. Although he alludes to some of the great philosophical and theological theories about mankind, his only answers to the problems and enigmas of life are age-old adages and cliches. He seems to feel that some answer is better than none, and he always chooses an answer which seems practical and at least makes sense within the framework of the experience of Grover's Corners. His philosophy of daily life is that the little events are the most important; his philosophy of love and marriage is traditional; his philosophy of death is unique and is really a philosophy of life since the dead pity the living who cannot fully appreciate life.

While he occasionally arranges props and directs the other players, his main role is that of narrator. He keeps the play moving by capsule summations and subtle hints about the future. This casualness is evident since he smokes a pipe, wears a hat, moves about the stage freely, greets and dismisses the audience at the beginning and end of each act, leans informally against the proscenium pillar, and enters and leaves the dialogue at will. As the moderator between the audience and the actors, he cuts short Professor Willard's remarks before they become overbearing yet he allows the proficient Mr. Webb to take as much time as he likes in answering questions. The Stage Manager also relates biographical, anecdotal, geographical and historical details about the characters as they enter and leave the action. His own philosophy occurs in his five major monologues, but he comments on a particular subject or incident almost anytime he wants to. For example, in Act I, after he relates the fact that Joe Crowell, Jr. went to college, did well and then died in World War I, he adds that all that education was for nothing. Or at the beginning of his role as minister in Act II, he explains he has assumed it because he's interested in the quality of mankind. In Act III, he winds his watch symbolically as the play closes.

DOCTOR FRANK GIBBS

Doc Gibbs, as he is known to his patients and most of the townspeople, is a country doctor in the best tradition of that profession. He always has a smile and good word for everyone he meets, and he is always genuinely solicitous of the welfare and improvement of his former patients. His life is dedicated to public service. After his vocation comes his family, with whom he has a magnificent relationship. He and his wife love each other deeply; theirs is indeed "a marriage of true minds." The doctor wastes few words, either with his patients or in disciplining his two children, George and Rebecca. His hobby is the Civil War and he knows enough about it to be considered an expert by his lifetime friend and next door neighbor, editor Webb. His charity is always evident; it is especially seen in his tolerant and patient attitude toward Simon Stimson, the town drunk.

The doctor is a master of the psychology of common sense with his son George. For example, let us consider a couple of the domestic crises which motivate "father-son" talks. The first occurs when George is shirking the responsibility of helping his mother with the chores, and in particular with the wood chopping. George is sixteen years old and his main interest is baseball. First of all, the father asks George how old he is and then what he plans to do for a living when he finishes school. George replies that he would like to be a farmer. Dr. Gibbs asks him if he would be willing to do all the hard work associated with farming. Of course, he has challenged George's teenage pride. The doctor now makes his point by indirectly painting a true picture of George's overworked mother who now has to chop the wood in addition to all her other obligations. George begins to cry. Then his father plays his high card - he raises George's allowance, not as a bribe but because George is getting older. George thanks his father, and, needless to say, the wood is chopped regularly for the next few years.

A second crisis occurs when George decides to get married. Dr. Gibbs cannot imagine his son being ready for such an important step. With a little just help from his wife, Frank Gibbs recalls that he wasn't very different from George when he married.

The doctor is very much in love with his wife, the former Julia Hersey. Julia constantly worries about the doctor ruining his health. She pleads with him to get enough sleep and take a vacation every two years, at which time he makes what can be considered almost a pilgrimage to the battlefields of the Civil War. His wife says that he's never as happy as when he's at Gettysburg or Antietam.

He and his wife are constantly kidding and teasing in the manner of frolicsome young lovers rather than people who have been married for twenty years. For example, he humorously chastises his wife for standing on the corner gossiping with a lot of old hens; when George is about to marry, he teases her by saying that she is losing one of her chicks; and finally he kids her about their never having run out of things to talk about in twenty years of marriage. They are a very affectionate couple who enjoy walking about their yard arm in arm under the moonlight.

It must have grieved him deeply to bury his loving wife nearly twenty years before he was to die. And then, only three years later, to bury his daughter-in-law Emily who had given him his first grandchild. Because his whole life was dedicated to the practice of medicine and to the service of mankind, the town named the new hospital after him when he died in 1930.

JOE CROWELL, JR.

The paperboy who delivers the morning *Grover's Corners Sentinel* rises about 5:45 each morning to do his job. A bright boy, he graduates first in his class at Grover's Corners High School. He wins a scholarship to Massachusetts Tech where again he is first in his class. He has a brilliant future ahead of him as an engineer, but he is killed in France during World War I. Joe's function in the play is to show the attitude of the Stage Manager after he relates the boy's biography. The Stage Manager is relating the ironic sequence of events (Joe's career and death) becomes bitter when he comments that all of Joe's education was for nothing. Joe's brother, Si, replaces him as the paperboy. Joe has a trick knee which many townspeople use to predict the weather.

HOWIE NEWSOME

Howie and Bessie, the imaginary horse which pulls his imaginary milkwagon, are both punctual and reliable. For instance, when the Lockharts move out of town, Bessie still stops in front of their house each morning. Howie is married and about thirty years old at the beginning of the play. Friendly, provincial, and chatty, he is a master of that type of early morning quiet conversation which tends to subtly inform and soothe the listener. Conversation is his main source of information, and probably one of the principal joys of his life.

JULIA GIBBS

Formerly Julia Hersey, of one of the town's oldest families, she is a loving mother and wife who dedicates her whole life to her family. She is also very kind to others, as can be seen by her defense of Simon Stimson to the gossip, Louella Soames. She is plump, pleasant and in her mid-thirties as the play begins.

Early in the play, Julia decides to sell a family antique in order to take the doctor on a vacation. But he will not go; in fact, he won't allow the subject to be discussed. She handles all the little discipline problems with the children and turns the major ones over to her husband. When we see her she is always doing something - sewing, cooking, washing dishes or clothes, feeding the chickens, etc. Her recreation comes from singing in the church choir. Her best friend and next door neighbor is Myrtle Webb.

Julia's motherly concern for her children is seen when she tells them to walk correctly; when she is on the point of tears just before George marries; and when she makes him wear his rubbers when he wants to visit Emily on the morning of the wedding. She projects most of her anxiety into her cooking. Her stove gives here strength and security many times.

Julia's strength is seen when she easily convinces George to go through with the marriage when he panics at the "altar-rail." Julia dies while visiting Canton, Ohio to see her daughter, Rebecca. She is buried on the hill in the Gibbs' plot. In the last act, she greets her young daughter-in-law and consoles her. They chat as if they were alive, and we learn that Julia left George and Emily the money she received for the antique she sold in Act I and planned to use for her husband's vacation. She knew he would never take one after she died. When Emily wishes to return to life for one day, Julia advises her against it, because it will make it more difficult to adjust to being dead. Mrs. Gibbs is given a front row seat in the cemetery and seems somewhat relieved after a busy life which she thoroughly enjoyed. She appears to be quite detached from the life in Grover's Corners which she once lived so vigorously. Her death occurred in 1910.

MYRTLE WEBB

Mrs. Webb is very much like her best friend and neighbor Julia Gibbs. In Act I, she is thin and crisp and younger than Mrs. Gibbs. They live next door to each other; they each have two children, a boy and a girl; their husbands are respected and well situated in the town; they own the same type of homes and they belong to the same church and sing in same choir. Mrs. Webb disciplines the children, especially in the table manners. One of her pleasant memories was when her husband took her to see the Atlantic Ocean. In her youth, she was the second prettiest girl in town next to Mamie Cartwright. She is one of the first people to notice that George and Emily are falling in love. She impresses the importance of humility upon Emily, and she values the health of her children above anything else.

She and Mrs. Gibbs share some of their household chores and most of their dreams and frustrations. Mrs. Webb is sympathetic to Simon Stimson's problems. On the day of the wedding she enforces the age-old tradition of the groom not seeing the bride. It is more difficult for her to let Emily go, and she hopes someone has told her something about being married. She thinks that it is cruel that girls have to enter marriage knowing so little about it. But her husband reminds her that she wasn't much older when they were married. As she is about to become exasperated, the ceremony begins.

Only a few years later she suffers great personal loss and sorrow when her son Wally dies on a camping trip with the Boy Scouts. Then, a few years after that, she loses her daughter Emily. The last we see of Mrs. Webb is at the wedding, although we know she is at Emily's funeral. Of course, we do see her in Act III when Emily relives her twelfth birthday, but the playwright spares us the terrible grief that this innocent and dedicated mother must have suffered by the deaths of her two children.

REBECCA GIBBS

At the age of eleven Rebecca is a vain little girl who announces to her mother that her main love in life is money. At fifteen, her father describes her as one who has to know and take part in everyone's business. She is one of the few characters in the play who desires to go beyond the limits of Grover's Corners. As she grows older she teases her brother George constantly, but her love for him is shown by her tears when she learns he is going to marry Emily and move out of the house. One evening she relates to George the strange address on a letter her friend Jane Crofut received from her minister. It was addressed to Jane Crofut, the farm on which she lived, the town, the county, the state, the country, the continent, the universe, and, finally, the mind of God. Both George and Rebecca are amazed by this, but only Rebecca realizes the romance and dimension that such an address gives to Grover's Corners. Eventually Rebecca marries an insurance man and settles in Canton, Ohio, fulfilling her desire to live in and experience another part of the world.

WALLY WEBB

A vibrant young boy, Wally tries to compete with his sister for good grades, but he concludes that he is only bright when it comes to his stamp collection. His mother constantly has to scold him for reading at the dinner table. Wally makes a great deal of fuss over the present that he has made in manual training class for Emily's twelfth birthday. He dies from a ruptured appendix while on a camping trip with the Boy Scouts.

PROFESSOR WILLARD

Unlike most of the other characters in the play, this professor from the state university is not emotionally involved in Grover's Corners. Therefore, his remarks are scientific and objective. They seem cold and pedantic in comparison to the descriptions of the town as given by the Stage Manager and editor Webb. He gives a geological and archaeological history of the town and then an anthropological history. The professor is the only character Wilder satirizes in the play. He calls him a rural scholar and has him so disoriented at the end of his report that the Stage Manager has to help him find his way off the stage. He wears glasses and reads his comments from lecture notes.

MR. CHARLES WEBB

Editor Webb, as he is so often called in the play, is the editor of *The Grover's Corners Sentinel,* a local paper which is published twice a week as the play begins but more regularly later on. He is a journalist of the old school, concerned with accuracy, detail, and avoiding as many printing errors as he can. He is a cultured and intelligent gentleman with a fine and proportioned sense of humor. He is a graduate of Hamilton College in New York State. Like Doc Gibbs, he is dedicated to his profession, his family, and to Grover's Corners.

He frankly answers the audience's questions on drinking, social issues, and culture early in the play (see Characters in the Audience). He dearly loves his son and daughter, and, like his wife, survives them both. One example of his concern for his son is seen when he asks Constable Warren to keep an eye on Wally's smoking. His close relationship with his daughter is shown on the day of her wedding. Whereas it is Mrs. Gibbs who gives George the strength when he becomes frightened at the wedding, it is Mr. Webb who supports his daughter when she is hesitant about the whole thing. In one of the funniest scenes in the play, Mr. Webb advises his future son-in-law about marriage. He offers George the same advice his father gave him many years before. It consists of a group of traditional male views built around the idea that the man is the boss. Then he tells George to do the same thing he did with the advice - ignore it - and he will be quite happy.

Mr. Webb is also sympathetic and charitable to Simon Stimson. He is close to his wife, and his best friend is Doc Gibbs.

His hobby is studying about Napoleon. Once again the audience is spared the grief this sensitive and gentle man must have suffered when he lost the son and daughter he loved so much.

CHARACTERS IN THE AUDIENCE

The Woman in the Balcony, the Man in the Auditorium, and the Lady in the Box, are all used to symbolize various social and political philosophies and causes. For example, The Woman in the Balcony inquires about drinking in Grover's Corners. Perhaps she represents Prohibition. The Man in the Auditorium is described as belligerent, and is anxious about social injustice and industrial inequality. He can easily be seen to represent the seething economic and political crises of the 1930s in this country. Some of these crises were manifested in the Red Scare, socialism, and labor violence. This man is more common to John Steinbeck's *Grapes of Wrath* and *In Dubious Battle* than to the works of Wilder. The Lady in the Box represents wealth and society. It follows that she is interested in culture and love of beauty. Editor Webb handles these three symbolic questioners in an interesting way. He answers the liquor question by understatement and anecdote: for example, he says that liquor is needed for snakebites. He is more direct in answering the question on social equality. According to the editor, those who work hard get somewhere; those who are lazy seldom get anywhere. At least that's the way it should be, but sometimes life rewards the lazy and seems to punish the industrious. People spend more time needlessly talking about injustice and luck than they spend actually doing something about it. The people of Grover's Corners, nevertheless, are always willing to help the needy. Editor Webb quietly evades the question on culture. With the exception that a few girls at the high school play the piano, and almost everyone in town reads the Bible and Robinson Crusoe and almost everyone in town is familiar with Handel's "Largo" and Whistler's "Mother," there isn't very much fine arts culture in Grover's Corners. One has the feeling that Editor Webb doesn't really think it's necessary for the good life, but he would be the last to describe the people here as "culturally deprived."

SIMON STIMSON

The organist at the Congregational Church, he also conducts the choir whose membership includes, among others, Mrs. Gibbs, Mrs. Webb, and Mrs. Soames. Simon loves music and considers that its purpose is to give pleasure. He constantly reminds his choir that loud singing is not necessary for good music. His humor is seen when he tells the members of the choir to leave the loud singing to the Methodists because the Congregationalists couldn't beat them even if they tried. Simon drinks a great deal, and has even been seen in church in a tipsy condition. Mrs. Soames thinks this is a public scandal and agitates for some action. Mrs. Gibbs as well as the whole town is aware of Simon's problem but they are willing to ignore it as long as possible because he has had many troubles. Dr. Ferguson, the minister, is also sympathetic to Simon's problems. Mrs. Gibbs charitably says that Simon is drinking less than he used to drink, but Mrs. Soames still feels just the opposite. Dr. Gibbs knows more about the causes of Simon's alcoholism than anyone else in town. But he only hints at the cause as he makes a general observation that some people just aren't meant for small-town life. There is little that can be done for Simon, so people try to ignore his problem. Even when Constable Warren sees Stimson's wife out looking for him, he looks the other way so he doesn't have to embarrass her. One evening Mr. Webb sees Simon stumbling down the street and offers to walk along with him (so he won't get hurt).

But Simon just stares at him and staggers along without saying anything. At the end of the play we learn that Simon committed suicide. His gravestone bears a unique **epitaph** - some notes of music. Although many characters mention that Simon had many troubles, we never learn precisely what they are. However, he did gain a certain amount of fame when a Boston newspaper ran an article about his unique **epitaph**. When we meet him among the dead he is bitter about life as might be expected. He sees man as the victim of one selfish passion or another, and feels that people are blind and ignorant. Simon Stimson is an interesting minor figure in the play. Comparing Edward Arlington Robinson's poetic characters, Simon is not as romantic as "Miniver Cheevy," but he is more like a "Mr. Flood" who follows "Richard Cory's" course of action. His function in the play is not to show the evils of alcoholism or suicide, but to reflect the Christian and charitable attitude the town shows him.

MRS. SOAMES

Louella Soames is an impolite busybody and gossip, who occasionally means well by her gibberish. We first see this when she wants Simon Stimson fired as church organist because he is drunk. Mr. Soames, it is hinted, is not very happy with his wife's carryings-on. Her impoliteness is seen at Emily and George's wedding when she is constantly chatting from the last pew in the church. He chatter is loud enough to drown out the minister. She also has the irritating habit of describing everything in trite superlatives, as "this is the loveliest wedding I ever saw." And, of course, she can be depended upon to say something of this nature loud enough for all to hear at every social function she attend. Louella does not change much after she dies. In the cemetery scene she again launches into a tirade of trite superlatives and **cliches** to review Emily's life. Ironically, and perhaps not without purpose, she has a second row seat to Simon Stimson in the cemetery.

CONSTABLE WARREN

The town's police officer, Constable Warren, is the epitome of the kindly small town or neighborhood cop. He knows everyone's name and habits, background and problems. More important, he knows how to treat everyone, especially the teenagers and children. His duties cover the whole spectrum of public safety, from flood control to crime. However, there is little crime in Grover's Corners. In fact, at the beginning of the play, most people do not even lock their doors at night. Although he is old, his memory is good enough to recall many details about Hank Todd, the baseball star of Grover's Corners some twenty years before. He tells us that Hank moved to Maine and eventually became a parson. Constable Warren shows humility when he rescues a drunk from freezing to death in a snowdrift, and declines from having it put in *The Grover's Corners Sentinel.* In another scene, he avoids embarrassing Mrs. Stimson when he looks the other way as she seeks her drunken husband. He knows enough about the nature of young boys in town that when Mr. Webb asks him to speak to his son about smoking, he tells the editor that Wally smokes no more than two or three cigarettes a year. The constable, as can be seen, is a fine and respected citizen of the community. We learn of his death from Emily.

THREE BASEBALL PLAYERS

George's three high school teammates unnecessarily and inappropriately tease him about his marriage to Emily. While their remarks are not blatantly improper they do border on indelicacy. They are quickly silenced by the State Manager who comments that our society is too advanced for such a primitive display of nonsense.

JOE STODDARD

The town undertaker. Joe tells Sam Craig that while death is his business and he should be used to it, he can't help feeling sad at Emily's funeral because she was so young. In walking through the cemetery, he talks in terms of how long ago he brought someone up here or in terms of what caused their death. He feels sorry for Doc Gibbs who buried his wife three years ago and will bury his daughter-in-law today. We also learn from Joe the story of Simon Stimson's suicide, his unique **epitaph**, that Emily died in childbirth, and that she and George have a four-year-old son. He also reminds us that new sections of the cemetery are opening all the time.

SAM CRAIG

Sam is a nephew of Julia Gibbs and returns after twelve years' absence from Grover's Corners for Emily's funeral. In a conversation with Joe Stoddard, the undertaker, he catches up on who has died since he left town. He relates that he is now in business in Buffalo, New York. As they walk through the cemetery Sam recalls many friends he had quickly forgotten until seeing their gravestones. He and Joe talk of Mrs. Gibbs, farmer McCarty, Simon Stimson, Emily, and Sam's parents. Sam is used to symbolize that the dead are soon forgotten, that many times a man only returns to his former home for a funeral, and that people are naturally provincial in their view of places outside their own areas. When he is introduced, the Stage

Manager tells us he is from out West, and later Sam tells Joe that since he was back East he came to the funeral. The expressions make Grover's Corners, New Hampshire, and Buffalo, New York seem thousands of miles away from each other rather than the few hundred miles which actually separates them.

GEORGE AND EMILY

George and Emily are the main characters of the play. They constitute a good portion of the action in Act I and most of the action in Acts II and III. They are always together. We do not learn until Act III that George was interested in Emily as early as the age of twelve when he avoided the embarrassment of a confrontation and left her birthday present on her back porch. George and Emily are the same ages, attend the same schools and the same church, and live in adjacent homes. In the play they progress from a normal teenage stage to a normal young adulthood. They are nonconformists and appear to have no particular anxiety when they think about their future. They are obedient and responsible children who have a wholesome relationship with their parents. The lines of communication between parent and child are always kept open for both of them. There is a certain amount of teasing and competition between George and his younger sister and Emily and her younger brother, but this appears to be a natural sibling rivalry. Both seem to have high moral standards. Emily, for instance, will not give George the complete algebra answers because that would be cheating, but she will give him some hints. When George buys Emily an ice cream soda and does not have the money to pay for it, he is willing to leave his watch with Mr. Morgan as collateral until he returns. Emily's anger at George's conceit is on a moral level. She feels that her father is perfect and George's father is perfect, so there's no reason why George can't be perfect.

In the first act, Emily is coming of age and is quite proud of her academic achievements but anxious about her looks. At this time George is only concerned with baseball and does not have time for Emily, schoolwork, or his chores. His immaturity is evident. For example, he doesn't feel awkward if he meets Emily accidentally while chasing a baseball; but he is only able to talk to her in very general terms in ordinary circumstances and barely musters the courage to ask her for help with his math homework. His growth shows as he is able to talk with her and relate his plans to become a farmer and to work on his Uncle Luke's farm. Emily is impressed by his ambition, but more so by his long-awaited attention.

The algebra assignments suffer as the two young people lose out to the romantic moonlight when they communicate each evening from their bedroom windows in the adjacent homes. George is elected president of the senior class and Emily is elected class secretary and treasurer, bringing the two into even closer contact. George suffers from what today is called "senioritis" - but what in 1911 or even now would be called a "big head." In one of the most sensitive scenes in the play, George and Emily make their decision to spend the rest of their lives together, appropriately while sipping ice cream sodas. George shows his rising maturity as he accepts Emily's criticism and decides that marrying her is more important than going to agricultural college. He speaks his romantic lines almost intuitively. Emily, on the other hand, who began the conversation with little conscious thought to marriage, accepts George's proposal with equal intuition. For the first time, George tells his teammates to play without him until he walks Emily home.

As a result of their youth, the emotional and intuitive decision to marry, and a human being's natural love for freedom, both George and Emily have second thoughts on the day of the wedding. But with the moral support of their parents they survive the mental anxieties of the wedding ceremony. As far as we know they enjoy success and happiness, but it would be foolish to think that they did not have their troubles. In the last act we learn of Emily's premature death.

George will probably never get over losing Emily as she gave birth to their second child. They also have a four-year-old boy. At the funeral, he again receives the moral strength to endure the sorrow from his father and the Webbs. However, when all the mourners are gone. George returns alone and kneels of Emily's grave; he cannot leave her, and it will probably take him a long time to learn to bear his sorrow. The scene can be compared to Edgar Allen Poe's famous lines in "Annabel Lee:"

But our love it was stronger by far than the love of those who were older than we - Of many far wiser then we - And neither the angels in heaven above Nor the demons down under the sea, Can ever dissever my soul from the soul Of the beautiful Annabel Lee.

Simultaneously with her burial, Emily joins the other dead seated in neatly arranged rows of chairs. There is an empty chair awaiting her arrival. George and Emily are ideally complementary personalities. Their lives had much joy and happiness until this sad ending. One can almost hear one of the townspeople saying before he goes to bed that night, "The Lord giveth and the Lord taketh, but we are never ready."

OUR TOWN

ESSAY QUESTIONS AND ANSWERS

....

Question: Why is *Our Town* called a presentational drama?

Answer: *Our Town* is a presentational drama because so many of the properties and much of the scenery usually associated with dramatic productions are absent in this play. The Stage Manager or the characters create images of the scenes necessary for the action of the play. Usually these images are visual, such as the Stage Manager's description of the churches, homes, and stores of Grover's Corners, but sometimes sound images are used. For example the sound of clanking bottles represents Howie Newsome's milk bottle rack, the train whistle is used to represent the 5:45 train for Boston, and the factory whistle to represent the Cartwright blanket factory.

The advantages of this dramatic technique are obvious. It frees the production from unnecessary encumbrances and focuses the audience's attention on the lines of the characters. In the few places where actual props are used, they are still largely presentational. For example George and Emily mounted on the tops of step ladders representing the second floor bedrooms would be meaningless unless we knew from the dialogue that they were going upstairs to study after supper. The same is true in the drugstore scene. George offers to buy Emily an ice cream soda at Mr. Morgan's drug store. Meanwhile, the Stage Manager, who also plays the druggist, places two high stools behind a board, which is resting on the backs of two chairs from the Gibbs' kitchen. Mr. Morgan scoops imaginary ice cream into imaginary glasses and draws imaginary soda from imaginary faucets. This presentational technique does not detract from the **realism** of the scene; in fact, it offers the audience fewer distractions so that the major emphasis is on the dialogue and acting. In his dramatic principles, Thornton Wilder cites "pretense" as one of the most important conditions for good drama; he successfully applies this principle in this play.

Question: How do we know that *Our Town* is really concerned with more than Grover's Corners, New Hampshire, in the early 1900s?

Answer: There are several ways in which the play shows us that its scope is wider than just the daily events of several ordinary people in a small New Hampshire town in the early 1900s. The most obvious way is through the monologues of the Stage Manager. While he is initially concerned with Grover's Corners or the characters, he constantly makes reference to other people and other places in order to give the play a larger dimension. He either proceeds from a particular observation or comment about someone or something in the town to a general statement about the condition of mankind, or he reverses this procedure and begins with a general statement about some aspect of human nature and then shows its application to a particular character or event in the play. For example, when he narrates and presides at George's and Emily's wedding, his initial comments range through the whole question of marriage. Why do we have the custom? How do two people decide they're ready to marry? What effect does it have on the relatives of the couple? And how do we know it will work? These are his major considerations. He also tells us that some people say the ceremony is a sacrament and others say its only a continuation of the rat race of life. He amplifies the seriousness of the act by discussing its spiritual aspects, by noting its tradition, and by alluding to some of the old wedding customs in ancient Rome. Certainly his remarks transcend the wedding of a particular couple in a particular place.

Another way used to give the drama universality is the size of the numbers used in describing series of events. In this way the series naturally becomes much larger than any ordinary happening. For instance, the Stage Manager describes a married couple in terms of eating 50,000 meals together, and tells us that afternoon is here because dinner has been eaten by, and the dishes have been washed for, all of Grover's Corners 2,642 citizens. Professor Willard reports that the land has been here for 200,000,000 or 300,000,000 years. The Stage Manager calls upon the millions and millions of people who have married throughout the history of man to be witnesses at George's and Emily's marriage. At another point he talks of the millions of people in ancient civilizations who had daily lives, yet how little we know about them. The play began in a specific place on a particular day and at a precise moment, but in the last lines of the drama there is a reference to the stars doing their old, old crisscrossing. The implication here is that there are many Grover's Corners and countless characters like those we have met in the play, who have, are, and will continue the cycles of daily life, love, marriage, procreation, and eventual death. The name of the play itself is indicative of its universality; it is indeed our town and the human predicament which is its purpose.

Question: At the conclusion of Act I, what is the significance of Jane Crofut's letter?

Answer: As the first act closes, Rebecca Gibbs tells her brother George about a uniquely addressed letter that Jane Crofut received from her minister when she was sick. The letter was addressed to "Jane Crofut, Crofut Farm, Grover's Corners, Sutton County, New Hampshire, U.S.A., Continent of North America, Western Hemisphere, the Earth, the Solar System, the Universe, the Mind of God." Rebecca and George are amazed that the letter was received since the total of their geographical experience probably never went beyond the county or at least the Eastern coast of the United States at this point of their lives. The significance of this unique address is Wilder's way of setting Grover's Corners in perspective with the rest of the world and even the universe and ultimately with God Himself. George and Rebecca know, like the majority of people, where they live. However, many times people fail to know their relationship to the larger areas around them. While the Crofut Farm and Grover's Corners and its citizens are microscopic in comparison to the universe and infinitesimal in comparison to God, they are, nevertheless, a part of both.

Question: What is the function of the Stage Manager?

Answer: Usually a stage manager is part of the non-acting personnel and, in most plays, he is in complete charge of the physical aspects of the production. In *Our Town,* the Stage Manager goes well beyond his usual function in a play and becomes a major performer. While he still arranges properties and does a limited amount of directing, his principal role is that of narrator. His informality in dress, manners, and speech sets the tone of the production. He makes several long speeches which give the audience the "pretenses," background, and ideas it needs to enjoy the production. He introduces the characters with brief biographical sketches and dismisses them when their dialogue is no longer necessary to the action. He opens and closes each act. His opening remarks take the place of the program as he lists the playwright, the producer, the actors, and all of the other information usually found in the written program.

In many ways he represents the community itself, and he appears sympathetic to the characters and their problems. He assumes several minor roles also. In Act I, he plays a woman in the street whom George has accidentally bumped into while chasing a baseball; in Act II, he plays Mr. Morgan, the druggist and the minister who performs the marriage ceremony; in Act III, he is Emily's contact between the living and the dead. Wilder used the technique of the Stage Manager as narrator and actor in some of his earlier one-act plays, but in *Our Town* he is elevated to the major position of the person who is most responsible for the play's success.

Question: Are George and Emily realistic characters?

Answer: These young people, whom we see develop through the awkwardness of pre-adolescence and the superficial confidence of teenagers, are quite realistic in many ways. Naturally they are greatly influenced by their parents and environment and the times in which they live. It probably would be unrealistic in this day and age of George not to go to college even if he were married, but in 1904 as steady job was as important as an education. We find that Emily is more mature than George, and as a result she is better in school and more serious in general. She expects George to be perfect, and his honest reply to this expectation is that he will try to be. Their conversations going and coming from school, their remarks about school and subjects, George's love of baseball, and Emily's anger at his conceit are all very natural reactions. They are both moral and sensitive, although George tries to hide his feelings more than Emily. They are popular in school and are elected to high class offices in their senior year. At home, they experience some of the usual problems that young people have with their parents. One of the few sad scenes in the play is when George grieves at Emily's grave. Like George and Emily, the scene is quite realistic.

Question: What is the purpose and meaning of *Our Town*?

Answer: *Our Town* is not just a portrait of a small New Hampshire community at the turn of the century. Rather it is a commentary on a particular aspect of life. In the play we experience the seeming dullness of everyday life in Act I, and then one of the archetypal highlights of life in Act II, namely, marriage. In Act III, we experience the great paradox of life - that man must die. Death is intensified in *Our Town* because Emily is so young when she dies. Yet this supports the theory that the quality of a person's life has little to do with the number of years a person lives. Emily enjoyed a good life by all our standards. Her parents were kind, understanding, and realistic. She was popular and did well in her studies. She married the man she loved and he loved her in return. George, her husband, was the local baseball hero and settled down to a sound financial future, eventually taking over his uncle's farm. They were happy, successful, very much in love, and had a child. Why then, we must ask, was the play not more bitter about her death? The answer is that death is an inevitable event in life and it is only foolish to be bitter over something that will happen anyway.

The purpose and meaning of the play are seen when Emily relives her twelfth birthday and returns to take her place among the dead for all eternity. She has now seen life in perspective and never had she seen it more clearly than this. The little insignificant events of daily life - a hug, a cup of coffee, a dress -take on great magnitude now that she can no longer experience them. When she asks the Stage Manager if anyone ever really appreciates life, he answers that the saints and poets do, sometimes. More than other people, the saints and poets have that rare gift of seeing life clearly and loving it dearly for man's imperfections as well as for his attempts at perfection. Emily feels sorry for George who is still at her graveside when she resumes her seat in the cemetery. Her sorrow is not because of her death but because George is still among the living and does not realize how precious life really is, especially the little daily events we all take for granted.

THE SKIN OF OUR TEETH

INTRODUCTION

In this play, first performed in 1942, Wilder attempts his most ambitious **theme** - a study of all human history - in three acts. The play had a successful run in this country and has been performed all over the world. It won the author his third Pulitzer Prize.

Many of the stage techniques are similar to those found in Our Town. Once again the play is highly presentational. The audience is called upon to create many of the properties, but its greatest collaboration is needed in understanding the dual and simultaneous development of the action. The dialogue is past and present at the same time; many of the lines not only apply to a character in a contemporary American setting but also apply to all men at all times, from the caveman to the astronaut.

A projection of slides which depict certain scenes in the play helps the audience to visualize the action. There is a Stage Manager but his role is much more limited than in Our Town. The same is true of audience participation. An announcer takes over the narrative of the Stage Manager. Miss Somerset, the actress who plays Sabina, steps in and out of her role whenever she feels she cannot say Sabina's lines. Finally, there is a certain atmosphere of fable in Act I where we encounter a talking and domesticated dinosaur and mammoth.

The following chart is helpful in guiding the reader. It tells the time of each act, what force is threatening to destroy mankind, and what the conflict is.

Time Destructive force Conflict ACT I Prehistoric Ice Man vs. Nature ACT II Biblical Flood Man vs. Moral Law ACT III Modern War Man vs. Man

The most important presentational element is that the play is taking place in New Jersey at the same time as one of the above periods in man's history. Act I, for example, talks of annihilation from ice, yet at the same time we have George Antrobus working in an office building in New York and experiencing the rigors of the average commuter. In Act II, the Antrobuses are at a **convention** in Atlantic City. In Act III, the conflict is war and the Antrobuses are trying to recover from it and build peace. It is interesting to note when Wilder wrote the play - at the beginning of World War II, several years before the atomic bomb or the hydrogen bomb. This is significant since it shows that survival is an archetypal experience - it has been a problem for all men in all ages. Ice, fire, flood, plague, and war have taken their toll, yet somehow man has survived and according to Wilder it has been "by the skin of our teeth." The playwright has acknowledged that some of his ideas for this play were taken from James Joyce's *Finnegan's Wake.*

INTRODUCTION TO THE CHARACTERS

(It should be remembered that the principal characters function on three levels: (1) as members of a middle-class American family living in New Jersey; (2) as Biblical figures; and (3) as universal types or symbols.)

George Antrobus: The head of the family.

Mrs. Antrobus: His wife.

Henry Antrobus: Their son.

Gladys Antrobus: Their daughter.

Sabina: Their maid.

Mr. Fitzpatrick: The stage manager.

Dinosaur, Mammoth: Symbols of prehistoric times.

Telegraph Boy.

Refugees from the cold.

Doctor Professor Moses, a judge Homer, a blind poet

Miss E. Muse Miss T. Muse

Miss M. Muse

Two Ushers

Two Drum Majorettes.

Fortune Teller.

Two Chair Pushers.

Six Conventioneers.

Broadcast Official.

Defeated Candidate.

Miss Somerset: The actress who plays Sabina.

Ivy: Her maid.

Mr. Tremayne: A retired Shakespearean actor.

Hester: The wardrobe mistress.

Fred Bailey: The head usher.

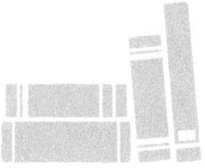

THE SKIN OF OUR TEETH

PLOT ANALYSIS

ACT I

Setting: The Antrobus Home in Excelsior, New Jersey.

Time: Contemporary and Prehistoric.

The play begins with an announcer broadcasting the news. He comments on several slides which are projected on a screen in front of the curtain. The slides include the sunrise, the front of the theater in which the play is being performed, the place in Vermont where a huge glacier is moving southward, the Excelsior, New Jersey home of Mr. and Mrs. George Antrobus, and several family shots. We are told that Mr. Antrobus is the inventor of the wheel and the lever, that he was once a gardener (Garden of Eden), that he is a veteran of foreign wars and that he has slowly worked his way up the ladder of success. The announcer tells us that Mrs. Antrobus is president of the local mother's club and invented the apron.

As the curtain rises, we view a typical commuter's home, and Sabina, the maid (whom Mr. Antrobus brought back from the Sabine Rape), gives a long soliloquy in which she describes Mr. Antrobus as the hunter who provides for the family and she hopes nothing will happen to him as he crosses the Hudson. She describes Mrs. Antrobus as a fine woman who has dedicated her life to the children to the exclusion of everything else. Sabina describes the Antrobus' son, Henry, as an average American teenager. Unintentionally she tells us that Henry, whose real name we learn is Cain, accidentally killed his older brother. Gladys, his sister, will make a good wife someday according to Sabina, although currently she is at the stage where she falls in love with movie stars. Sabina is very worried about the unusual cold in August and danger of the ice, but she concludes that the family has survived the dangers of dinosaurs, the plagues of locusts, and the depression, so they'll probably survive this crisis once again by the skin of their teeth. At the end of her soliloquy, Sabina tells us that she doesn't understand the play very well, but it's about the troubles the human race has experienced.

As Mrs. Antrobus enters, she is upset because Sabina let the fire go out. Sabina gives her notice because she can't stand the children and Mr. Antrobus pinches her. But Mrs. Antrobus ignores her request and is more concerned with the cold. They discuss Mr. Antrobus, and Sabina says that he is a great man and his wife doesn't appreciate it - especially his attempts to discover the alphabet and the multiplication tables. As Mrs. Antrobus is shooing away the dinosaur, a telegram arrives from her husband. Trying to get warm, the dinosaur and mammoth come into the house with the telegraph boy, who lights a fire for Mrs. Antrobus and Sabina. The telegram says burn everything but Shakespeare to keep the house warm. It also says that George is making good progress on the alphabet and the multiplication tables.

Mrs. Antrobus calls Gladys and Henry. She continually tells Gladys to act like a lady and she continually tells Henry not to throw stones. As Mr. Antrobus arrives home, he is carrying food parcels, a stone wheel, and a railroad lantern. A mood of anxiety pervades the whole group as it continues to get colder. Much to his wife's dismay, George takes in some refugees, including a judge named Moses, a blind poet named Homer, a professor who helped with the alphabet, and several Muses (symbolic of the arts and sciences). The refugees sing "Jingle Bells" while George attempts to teach his son the multiplication table, and Mrs. Antrobus teaches her daughter the Bible. As the first act ends, Mrs. Antrobus quotes Genesis, the glacier advances toward Excelsior, and the audience is asked to pass up its chairs to keep a fire going so that the human race can be saved.

Comment

It is evident that the characters are allegorical, not only in this first act but in the next two also. George, for example, is an average businessman and commuter who is a good provider. His family is dependent on him. On a larger level he symbolizes man's intelligence and ingenuity. He is also Adam, the first man, and his wife can be considered Eve. At the very beginning of the act we are told by the announcer that the cleaning women in the theater have found a wedding ring inscribed "To Eve from Adam. Genesis II:18."

In keeping with the primitive aspect in the dual development of the action in this act, the characters are concerned with the basic needs of life - is there a fire for warmth, will George get home safely, should we migrate because of the danger of the ice, will we have enough food? Mr. Antrobus' inventions are basic ones - the wheel, the lever, the alphabet, a number system.

The laws of Moses, the Bible, and Homer also seem to be three aspects of man's culture which will survive the glacier. The general **theme** of Act I is that the daily events of our lives are archetypal and that mankind has survived the Ice Age, volcanic eruptions, plagues, earthquakes, and other geological disorders by the skin of its teeth.

ACT II

Setting: Atlantic City Boardwalk.

Time: Biblical and 1942.

In this act the Antrobuses attend the 600,000th **convention** of mammals, subdivision humans, at Atlantic City. An announcer introduces George, who has just been elected president of the group. In his address George states that the **theme** for this year is "Enjoy Yourselves." When Mrs. Antrobus is asked to comment on her 5,000th wedding anniversary, she recalls the old days when there were no weddings. She relates that after a hard struggle women finally won the marital crusade and also the battle for wedding rings.

Sabina, who has been transformed into Miss Lily-Sabina Fairweather, hostess of the Boardwalk Bingo Parlor, is named Miss Atlantic City of 1942. With her mother, a fortune teller (symbolizing chance), she plots to seduce George and take him away from his family. Her plan almost succeeds, but is interrupted when George flees before the flood. He also takes his family, Sabina, and two of every type of animal. During the act we notice the effect of the worldly atmosphere on George, Gladys, and the other conventioneers. Atlantic City is portrayed as a modern Sodom and Gomorrah. Henry, as usual, causes trouble when he throws a stone at a man. As George, a modern day Noah, sails safely before the deluge, the fortune teller cautions him to think as he builds a new world.

Comment

In this act American conventioneers are humorously satirized. The happy, pleasurable days prophesied in George Antrobus' presidential speech are short lived as the vice-ridden and materialistic city and its fortune tellers and bingo parlors are destroyed by the flood. Lily-Sabina Fairweather loses that personality in the foul weather and returns to her role as the Antrobus' maid in order to be saved. The crisis also causes George to forget Miss Fairweather and concern himself with his family. Once again the human race manages to survive by the skin of its teeth. The parallels between the characters in this act and those in the Bible include George Antrobus as Noah, Mrs. Antrobus as Noah's wife, and Sabina (Lily-Sabina Fairweather) as Lilith, a symbol of seductive, sinful love as opposed to marital love.

ACT III

As she did in Act I, Sabina opens this last act with a soliloquy on what has passed. For several years she has been a camp follower. The Antrobus home has been partially destroyed during the war. She has seen Mr. Antrobus downtown talking up a recipe for grass soup. He is still inventive and interested in helping his fellow man. Mrs. Antrobus and Gladys, who has had a baby, come out of hiding. A war-fatigued, bitter, and hostile Henry, who has risen to the rank of general, comes home. He is disappointed that the war has ended. Like Hitler, he wants to burn all his father's books because that is where all the bad ideas come from. The family begins the difficult task of reconstruction. Slowly the symbols, machinery, and attitudes of war are replaced by those of peace. Everyone is relieved to get back to the dull routines of daily life. When George Antrobus returns home he fights with Henry. George symbolizes peace, creativity, and progress; Henry symbolizes the "Rebel Without A Cause," who hates for the sake of hate and wants to destroy the world for no particular purpose. George tells his son that he will always oppose that aspect of human nature for which his son stands. The father accepts some of the responsibility for the way Henry has turned out, and try as they might, it will be difficult to live in peace.

War weary and wounded, George lacks the energy to begin again. But encouraged by his wife and even Sabina, George resolves to continue the three things he feels are most important in life - the needs of people, the welfare of his family, and the tradition of ideas in his books, a few of which have been saved. In the last part of the play he alludes to quotations from Spinoza and Plato. The first emphasizes mind over matter and the second points out the importance of personal order before public or governmental order. A final **allusion** is to the beginning of Genesis, as man begins another portion in the cycle of his history.

Comment

Wilder has brought the history of man full cycle in this act. The conflict of our day, as it has been for the last four hundred years, is man against man. It is also in this act that the characters achieve universal dimension. George Antrobus is the type of man who will never lose his faith in man just as Mrs. Antrobus will never lose faith in her children. Ironically Henry's killer instinct has seen him rise from a corporal to a general in the war, and Gladys, following in her mother's footsteps, will raise the next generation. Chances are that her children will also survive by the skin of their teeth, with a few books and creeds to guide them, but always with the dual elements of good (George) and evil (Henry) in their personalities.

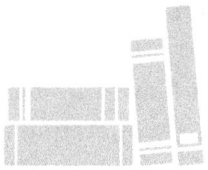

THE SKIN OF OUR TEETH

CHARACTER ANALYSES

GEORGE ANTROBUS

George symbolizes many phases and types of mankind in the play. Among these are the hunter, the provider, an inventor, a philosopher, Adam, Noah, a peace loving man who is willing to fight for his beliefs if it is necessary to do so, a successful businessman, a pillar of the church, and a man dedicated to the services of his fellow man and his family. He knows his own shortcomings as well as those of his son, and he tries to do his best in keeping peace. Humanity, his family, and his books are the three important things in his life.

MRS. ANTROBUS

George's wife, she symbolizes both the positive and the negative aspects of motherhood. She gladly sacrifices all her personal pleasures for her two children, Gladys and Henry. But on the negative side she is overprotective, a poor disciplinarian, and lacks the insight to see her children as they really are, especially Henry, for whom she always makes excuses. As an American, she stands for the suburban housewife and club woman. But as a final comment we can use a quotation from Hawthorne: "What wonderous strength and generosity is a woman's heart."

SABINA

The symbol of the temptress in the tradition of Helen of Troy, Cleopatra, and Lilith, Sabina is always disappointed as she loses George's affection. As a maid she is pessimistic, superstitious and goes through life out of habit with little real insight into it.

HENRY ANTROBUS

A rebel without a cause, Henry, who was once named Cain, is ironically against all the good things which his father represents. His misanthropy earns him the rank of general during the war.

GLADYS ANTROBUS

A fickle, easily misled girl, Gladys resembles her mother. She bears a child during the war to begin a new generation.

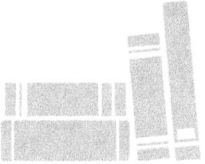

THE SKIN OF OUR TEETH

ESSAY QUESTIONS AND ANSWERS

Question: Discuss the play's comment on the history, development, and condition of mankind.

Answer: The play certainly demonstrates that man has had a turbulent history. The chronological pattern of development, geological in Act I, Biblical in Act II, and historic in Act III, point out three of many of the major phases of human history. The action in each of these phases and acts centers around man's conflict with nature, man's conflict with morality, and finally man's conflict with himself. In each phase, man has survived "by the skin of his teeth." The Antrobuses are not only Americans but stand for all mankind as well. Of course, Sabina says in the last lines of the play, there is no real end to the play since the history of man is a continual thing, but there is a general impression that the same cycle will repeat itself in future ages. Man advances to a certain point, then some conflict destroys much of his progress, but there are always a few to carry on - to begin to build again. Such restoration is due to the humanism and faith of men like George Antrobus who always seems to rise to the occasion. The play seems optimistic for the most part; it expresses the belief that mankind, despite the forces which threaten to destroy him, will, to use a phrase from William Faulkner's Nobel Prize Acceptance Speech, "endure and prevail."

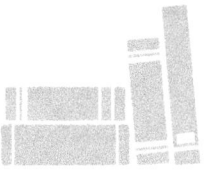

THORNTON WILDER

CRITICAL OPINION

SURVEY OF CRITICAL OPINION OF THORNTON WILDER

Most critics agree that Wilder's two most significant works are *Our Town* and *The Bridge of San Luis Rey*. Some drama critics, such as John Gassner, feel that the end of *Our Town* weakens it, but even from the first "it received enthusiastic comments from the critics and tumultuous applause from the audience," according to William Lyon Phelps. Its continued popularity, especially among amateur groups, marks it as Wilder's most successful work, even if particular critics lean toward other works. Rex Burbank, in his full length study of Wilder, cites *The Bridge of San Luis Rey, Heaven's My Destination,* and *Our Town* as the author's best works. Burbank feels that *The Skin of Our Teeth* falls short when compared to the others because it tends to become **didactic** and bathetic.

Critics Malcolm Cowley and Granville Hicks have suggested that the problem of Wilder and criticism is due principally to the fact that Wilder is difficult to place in any exact classification - he fits no particular niche. He writes well in three distinct **genres** - the novel, the play, and criticism. He differs from his contemporaries in his treatment of time (whereas they are specific and present, he is general and historical) and setting (whereas they write of particular geographical locations, he ranges the world). Both Cowley and Hicks feel that Wilder will be read as long as his contemporaries.

NEGATIVE CRITICISM

Throughout Wilder's career, he has been criticized heavily for two things: first, for not dealing with the social, economic, and historical crises of his day as his contemporaries did, and, second, for depending too heavily on the work of other literary artists as the sources for his novels and plays. In October, 1930, Michael Gold published an article in the *New Republic* entitled, "Wilder, Prophet of the Genteel Christ." Gold termed Wilder "an Emily Post of Culture" because he did not write directly of the horrors and tragedy of the widespread depression in America. This blistering attack had been overstated, and when the air cleared, the astute Malcolm Cowley candidly observed several years later that Wilder did not ignore the American crises but was more concerned with moral problems. "America's problems were moral ones," commented Mr. Cowley in his Exiles Return. Critics Henry Hazlitt and Edmund Wilson and scores of letter writers also defended Wilder against the emotional and unjust attack.

The second major criticism against Wilder - that he leans too heavily on source material - was answered by Wilder himself in his "Preface to Three Plays" in 1957. He clearly stated his indebtedness to Dante for the technique of the final act of *Our Town* and to James Joyce's *Finnegan's Wake* for many of the ideas in *The Skin of Our Teeth*. Critics have been quick to point out the many sources and parallels in these and earlier works. For example, critics have shown the parallels between *The Bridge of San Luis Rey* and Prosper Merimee's *Le Carrosse du*

Saint Sacrement, and the parallels in Johann Nestroy's comedy and *The Matchmaker.* Wilder himself, in an introductory note to *The Woman of Andros,* mentions his indebtedness to the Roman playwright, Terence. But while Wilder uses these sources as a beginning, the end result is usually distinctly his own.

AFFIRMATIVE CRITICISM

Wilder has an impressive list of critics in his corner. Among these are Edmund Fuller, Edmund Wilson, Malcolm Cowley, and Granville Hicks. These men praise Wilder as a master craftsman in his prose style, as an innovator in his drama, as one of the few writers in his age who achieves an archetypal perspective, and as a representative of the American moral tradition more familiar to the last century than to our own. Unlike his contemporaries, Wilder did not feel the necessity of revolting against tradition whether it be moral or political. There is no doubt that this morality and classicism made him less popular than Hemingway, Faulkner, Dos Passos, or Steinbeck during the 1930s and 1940s, but his principal efforts seem to have endured with that same style and message.

Wilder's productivity has also been slim compared to many of his fellow writers - all told, he has published five novels, four plays, and two collections of one-act plays. There is an accord among these critics that Wilder's works will endure because of his style, his humanism, and his overall **theme** of "love" in all its dimensions. That man will survive despite internal conflicts is symbolized by George Brush in *Heaven's My Destination;* that he will survive despite external conflicts is symbolized by George Antrobus in *The Skin of Our Teeth.* Between birth and death, the most important occurrence is "love," that aspect of human nature which according to Wilder gives life its most meaningful and lasting quality. Most of Wilder's philosophy is synthesized in *The Bridge of San Luis Rey* where the love is of another human being, and in *Our Town* where the love of life is the dominant theme.

WILDER AND THE CRITICS

Wilder waited for many years before he answered in a very general and oblique way the two chief criticisms which had been raised against his writings. In 1957 he wrote "Preface to Three Plays," in which he answered the criticism of ignoring contemporary American problems by telling about the success of *The Skin of Our Teeth* in postwar Germany and by once and for all stating that *Our Town* is a symbol of the human condition celebrating three of its most important characteristics - daily life, marriage, and death. Also in this preface, Wilder emphatically acknowledged his debt to James Joyce for some of the ideas and techniques used in *The Skin of Our Teeth*.

This short preface is destined to become the most famous of all Wilder criticism. It is interesting that Wilder, the critic, should write of Wilder, the artist. Fortunately, he also had the benefit of nearly thirty-one years in the literary workshop. In his last remarks in this short piece, he relates his famous analogy that literature is a torch race, and that he is not original but merely one of the many runners. In this one statement he dispels any criticisms which can be raised against his lack of originality, but, more important, it expresses his literary philosophy that all time is one time, and affirms his belief that all human activity is archetypal. His humor is obvious as he says that he had enjoyed his leg of the race. Finally his humanism, the influence of his teaching career, and his sense of the continuum of history is clearly seen when he says: "I should be very happy, if, in the future some author should feel similarly indebted to any work of mine."

THORNTON WILDER

SUGGESTED RESEARCH PAPER TOPICS

The length of these research papers can be determined in most instances by the number of Wilder's works the student wishes to treat in his study. Reference to the standard sources cited in the Bibliography is a good starting point. Adapt the suggested topic to your own requirements.

1. The influence of Classicism on Wilder.

2. The influence of religion on Wilder.

3. Wilder's metamorphosis from novelist to playwright.

4. The evolution of the role of Stage Manager from the one-act plays to *Our Town*.

5. The influence of setting in Wilder.

6. Criticize one of Wilder's plays according to his own dramatic philosophy as set forth in "Some Thoughts on Playwriting."

7. Wilder and the critics.

8. Discuss anti-intellectualism and idealism in *Our Town*.

9. Wilder's humanism.

10. Explicate the **allusions** in one of Wilder's works.

11. Wilder: Experimentor in the drama.

12. The influence of music on Wilder.

13. Female characters in Wilder.

14. Male characters in Wilder.

15. Foreign characters in Wilder.

16. Clerical characters in Wilder.

17. Wilder's style.

18. Wilder's technique of characterization.

19. Structure in Wilder's novels.

20. Structure in the one-act plays.

21. Parallels in the one-act plays and later works.

22. Point of view in Wilder's novels.

23. Practical problems in staging one of Wilder's plays.

24. Biographical sources in Wilder's works.

25. Wilder and his contemporaries.

26. Wilder as teacher and translator.

27. Wilder's career before *Our Town*.

28. Wilder's career since *Our Town*.

29. Wilder's influence on later authors.

30. Compare Wilder and one other novelist or playwright

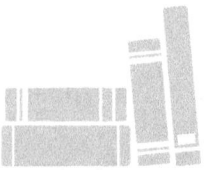

BIBLIOGRAPHY

For a checklist of Wilder criticism see Henry Kosok's "Thornton Wilder: A bibliography of Criticism" in *Twentieth Century Criticism* (Number IX, 1963). The best general article appraising Wilder's place in American letters is Edmund Fuller's "Thornton Wilder: The Notation of the Heart" in the *American Scholar* (Spring, 1959). An interesting article on the significance of *Our Town* can be found in the *English Journal* (May, 1956) and a rebuttal appears in *Modern Drama* (February, 1959).

Burbank, Rex. *Thornton Wilder.* New York: Twayne Publishers, Inc., 1961. The best full length study of Wilder. Mr. Burbank emphasizes Wilder's humanism.

Cowley, Malcolm. *Exiles Return.* New York: The Viking Press, 1951. A classic on Wilder's 1920s contemporaries.

——— *Introduction to A Thornton Wilder Trio.* New York: Criterion Books, Inc., 1956, 1-19. A general appraisal of Wilder's career, with unique biographical details.

Downer, Alan S. "A Revolt from Broadway," in *A Time of Harvest: American Literature 1910-1960*, ed. Robert E. Spiller. New York: Hill and Wang, 1962, 42-53. The effect of Eugene O'Neil, Maxwell Anderson, Phillip Barry, and Thornton Wilder on American Drama.

Fuller, Edmund. "Preface and Afterwords to *The Bridge of San Luis Rey*" in *Four American Novels*, ed. Edmund Fuller and Olga Achtenhagen. New York: Harcourt, Brace and Co., 1959, 586, 653-656. A fine critical commentary on the characters, **theme**, and style of the novel.

Fuller, Edmund and Kinnick, B. Jo. "*Our Town* An Afterword" in *Adventures in American Literature*. (Laureate Edition) ed. Mary Reeves Bowman. New York: Harcourt, Brace and World, 1963, II, 326-329. A discussion of the universality and the **theme** of the play.

Wilder, Thornton. "Preface to *Three Plays*." New York: Bantam 1961, VII-XII. The author's own view on *Our Town*, *The Skin of Our Teeth*, and *The Matchmaker*; also he states his philosophy of writing.

——— "Some Thoughts on Playwriting" in *Our Town*. New York: Harper Colophon Books, 1960, 105-108. A 1941 article in which Wilder states his theories on drama.

www.ingramcontent.com/pod-product-compliance
Lightning Source LLC
LaVergne TN
LVHW011709060526
838200LV00051B/2827